DEMOCRACY AND ECONOMIC POWER

DEMOCRACY AND ECONOMIC POWER

Extending the ESOP Revolution Through Binary Economics

Louis O. Kelso
and
Patricia Hetter Kelso

UNIVERSITY
PRESS OF
AMERICA

Lanham • New York • London

The Kelso Institute
for the Study of Economic
Systems

San Francisco

Copyright © 1986, 1991 by Louis O. Kelso and Patricia Hetter Kelso
University Press of America,® Inc.
4720 Boston Way
Lanham, Maryland 20706

3 Henrietta Street
London WC2E 8LU England

This edition was reprinted in 1991 by arrangement
with the authors and University Press of America, Inc.
and co-published by arrangement with the Kelso Institute
for the Study of Economic Systems

Library of Congress Cataloging-in-Publication Data

Kelso, Louis O.
Democracy and economic power : extending the ESOP revolution
through binary economics / Louis O. Kelso, Particia Hetter Kelso.
p.   cm.
Reprint. Originally published: Cambridge, Mass. :
Ballinger Pub. Co., ©1986.
Includes index.
1. Industrial management—United States—Employee participation.
2. Employee ownership—United States.
3. Trade-unions—Economic aspects—United States.
4. Income distribution—United States.
I. Kelso, Patricia Hetter. II. Title.
[HD5660.U5K45 1991] 338.6—dc20 90-20274 CIP

ISBN 0–8191–7908–6 (alk. paper).
ISBN 0–8191–7909–4 (pbk.: alk. paper).

 The paper used in this publication meets the minimum requirements of
American National Standard for Information Sciences—Permanence
of Paper for Printed Library Materials, ANSI Z39.48–1984.

To Christina, Trevor, and Julie, with renewed hope

Contents

List of Figures ix

Acknowledgments xi

Introduction: The Search for the Obvious Intensifies xv

PART I   UNDERSTANDING ECONOMIC DEMOCRACY

1   The Search for the Obvious 3
2   Democracy's Missing Half 11
3   The Concept of Democratic Capitalism 23
4   Say's Law Reconsidered 31
5   An Analysis of Conventional Finance 39

PART II   GETTING THERE

6   Financing Tools for Democratizing Capitalism 51
7   The ESOP, MUSOP, and CSOP 59
8   The GSOP 75
9   The ICOP, COMCOP, and PUBCOP 85
10 The RECOP 99
11 The Missing Logic of Finance: Commercially
    Insured Capital Credit 105
12 Democratizing the Business Corporation 117

PART III   UNIONS' NEW ROLE

13 The Unions' Role in Democratizing Capitalism 135
14 Do Labor Unions Have a Future? 141
15 The ESOP: Prime Tool for the New Producers'
    Unions 151

Glossary 165
Index 171
About the Authors 177

List of Figures

4-1   Say's Law as Applied to a National Economy   32
4-2   Say's Law Corrected to Recognize Both Labor
      Work and Capital Work   35

7-1   The Employee Stock Ownership Plan (ESOP)   60
7-2   The Mutual Stock Ownership Plan (MUSOP)   68
7-3   The Consumer Stock Ownership Plan (CSOP)   71

8-1   The AGSOC Purchase of the Interest of BP
      Pipeline, Inc. in the TransAlaska Pipeline (TAPS)   77

9-1   The Individual Capital Ownership Plan (ICOP)   87
9-2   The Commercial Capital Ownership Plan
      (COMCOP)   91
9-3   The Public Capital Ownership Plan (PUBCOP)   94

10-1 The Residential Capital Ownership Plan (RECOP)   101

11-1 Democratic Commercially Insured Contract
      Financing of Capital Transactions   107

12-1 Changing Participation of Labor and Capital
      Workers in Production of Goods and Services
      in the U.S. Economy   126

Acknowledgments

A basic truth is not invented but discovered. The more basic and universal it is, the more obvious it is apt to be and the harder to perceive, even though, like Poe's purloined letter, it lies in full view. Once found, its existence seems natural and inevitable. Everyone silently thinks, "How could I have missed that?"

Such a basic truth is the nucleus of this book.

Two-factor economics began as a young man's insight in the depths of the Great Depression. It grew into a manuscript entitled "The Fallacy of Full Employment," which happened to be completed just at the end of World War II when the Full Employment Bill of 1945 was on the verge of becoming law. If it is true that nothing is as powerful as an idea whose time has come, it is equally true that an idea whose time has not come will get no hearing. The manuscript was quietly put away until 1958 when Mortimer Adler persuaded the author to join with him and publish its essentials as *The Capitalist Manifesto.*

The Capitalist Manifesto asked Americans who thought they had solved the economy's income distribution problem through the mixed capitalist-socialist economy to think again about the implications of distributing through labor the ever growing stream of capital-produced income, as contemplated by the nation's official economic policy. In 1961, *The New Capitalists* criticized savings-based finance and proposed a financed capitalist plan. In 1967 *Two-Factor Theory: The Economics of Reality* launched the Employee Stock Ownership Plan (ESOP) movement. But still the investment banking world remained largely oblivious to the challenge of expanding America's ownership base—democratizing its economic power—until our founding of Kelso & Company in 1970.

Almost as frustrating as identifying a new basic idea is giving it the right name. In a field as old as political economics, such basic terms as democracy, capitalism, market, factors of production, etc., are not only scholarly property but encrusted with meanings and associations. Should an innovator make up a new term or stretch the meaning of an established one? In succession we used—then discarded: the theory of capitalism, capital theory, two-factor theory, Second Income Plan, universal capitalism, social capitalism and democratic capitalism.

Finally, the term for which we had been searching for almost 50 years announced itself: "binary economics." But this did not occur until after *Democracy and Economic Power* had been published. There is no gainsaying, however, that it is the right term. It implies that the labor theory of value, explicit in classic economics, implicit in modern, no longer fits the facts; that capital instruments must be recognized equally with labor as an input factor, thus transforming economics from a mono-system to a binary one.

We are greatly indebted to Kelso & Company, especially to its president and chief executive officer, Joseph Schuchert, and to our colleagues and staff in the firm for so ably carrying on the investment banking operations that have taken the ownership revolution into the business and financial world. Without their encouragement and support, we would not have been able to devote our energies to the writing of this book.

We are also indebted to Senator Russell B. Long, for many years the chairman of the Senate Finance Committee, whose leadership in Congress resulted in greatly facilitating ESOP financing.

William E. Chatlos, one of America's leading corporate strategists, has been a steadfast counselor and friend. Our gratitude to him is unending. Joseph Recinos, who has labored tirelessly to introduce the democratization of economic power into Latin America, is another who has never faltered.

Our super-competent writing assistants, Cynthia Hendershott Egan and Karen Buchea Cravotto, have both shared our labors and lightened them. Our original editors at Ballinger, Marjorie Richman and Barbara Roth, gave us such wise and painstaking guidance in developing our manuscript that we look upon them as collaborators in this effort.

Louis O. Kelso
Patricia Hetter Kelso
San Francisco
July 1990

The Search for the Obvious Intensifies

After 70 years of trying to make its government-owned, centrally planned economy work, the Soviet Union has formally abandoned the effort. Upon the ashes of the failed Marxist-Leninist economic experiment, the Soviets and the equally disillusioned Eastern Europeans are planning to construct the only other apparent alternative, a private-property, free-market economy.

The West not unnaturally interprets this astonishing conversion as a pragmatic and ideological victory for the economic system which the Marxist-Leninists vowed to destroy, and for most of the present century, did their best to destroy. It has magnanimously dispatched cadres of free-market missionaries—bankers, economists, accountants, lawyers, marketers, stockbrokers, communicators and various other presumably indispensable professional talents—to rehabilitate the fallen Marxists. Indeed, President Bush has proposed that the United States organize task forces for this altruistic undertaking.

But the Western market economies, enviable as they may seem to those still mired in varying stages of preindustrial poverty or post-industrial socialist poverty, are not successful working models for large and growing numbers of their own citizens. Not only have they not eradicated the chronic poverty that has always shadowed the base of the social pyramid, poverty is now beginning to claim growing numbers of the middle classes. The United States Government estimated that in 1989, 36 million people were below the poverty threshold of $11,611 for a family of four. The proportion of New Yorkers classified as poor has risen from 15 percent in the mid-1970s to 25 percent today.[1] And we must keep

1. *San Francisco Examiner*, March 12, 1989, p. 1.

in mind that government, not the people themselves, defines poverty in such a way as to keep the poor as invisible as possible.

It is now expected that mothers of small children will have to work outside the home. Two or more incomes are necessary to attain the standard of living a single breadwinner once could command. In 1950, seven out of ten Americans could afford an average new home.[2] In 1970, the Secretary of Housing and Urban Development estimated that 80 percent of the American people could not afford to buy a new home.[3] As the 1990s open, uncounted millions of Americans are homeless—among them an admitted one million children.

That "poverty is the mother of crime," as the Roman historian Marcus Aurelius Cassiodorus pointed out, has been recognized since antiquity. In 1987, almost three and one-half million adults were under the custody of federal, state and local correctional authorities, including men and women in prisons and jails—almost 2 percent of the nation's adult population. A Justice Department official (Joseph Bessette, acting director, Bureau of Justice Statistics, an arm of the Justice Department) estimated that one out of every 53 adults in the United States was under some form of correctional supervision on any given day in 1987. The number of adults in the U.S. on parole rose 11 percent from 1986–87.[4]

But the most incontrovertible evidence of the traditional market economy's unworkability is provided by the diverse and growing deficits—federal budget deficit, trade deficit, city, county and state budget deficits—which are making it increasingly impossible for governments at every level to function. As we write, the United States budget deficit is estimated as in the range of $184 to 206 billion for the 1991 fiscal year, augmenting a three trillion dollar national debt and off-balance sheet liabilities of over $10 trillion.[5]

A successful market economy has no permanent deficits, neither budget nor trade. Deficits arise from the economy's ina-

---

2. *Fortune,* "Is the One-Family House Becoming a Fossil? Far From it," April, 1978, p. 85.
3. Mike Mansfield, Senator from Montana, Senate Majority Leader, in an address delivered on NBC radio and television, June 24, 1970, reported in *U.S. News & World Report,* July 6, 1970, p. 68.
4. *San Francisco Chronicle,* November 14, 1988, p. A-8.
5. *The Economist,* "Apocalypse Soonish," June 2, 1990, p. 80.

bility or failure to operate on current account. Why, then, does debt in the U.S. and in other Western economies so relentlessly soar? Because, as the poverty statistics show, growing numbers of people cannot earn, from legitimate participation in production, enough income to support themselves and their families. Inadequate personal and family incomes translate into inadequate purchasing power in the national economy. Ever since the Great Depression, Western democratically-elected governments have understood that they are ultimately responsible for their economy's prosperity. When poverty reaches a point where it can no longer be ignored, portending yet another depression, the government is obliged to act. Redistribution, always government's last resort, is now its primary tool for managing the economy and staving off economic collapse.

The key means of redistribution is taxation—more than half of the U.S. tax harvest (state, municipal and federal) is used for transfer payments, open or disguised—supplemented by labor and social policies that override free-market forces and require higher and higher pay for less and less work input. These have destroyed and continue to destroy both competitiveness and product quality in industries across the board. But taxation, as a French tax collector once explained, is the art of plucking the goose so as to get the most feathers with the least hissing. The American people are loathe to part with their earnings and income, or to allow the institution of private property to erode beyond a certain point. What governments cannot obtain from taxpayers, they make up through borrowing. Thus the fatal deficits are born and begin to undermine solvency.

It is clear that present market economies are subject to internal limitations that prevent them from spontaneously generating the powerful (i.e., prosperous) consumers required under free-market principles to support a powerful productive sector. They must rely heavily on synthetic demand resulting from various forms of subsidized production, of which the most sinister is military boondoggle. A major and growing segment of the population simply cannot earn in the marketplace the incomes they need either to support the prosperity of the producers or a good economic life for themselves. Either market theory no longer works in the post-industrial world, or something profound has been overlooked.

But now both taxation and redistribution have reached their limits in the U.S. economy. The size of the budget deficit and its implications have paralyzed Congress. Somehow money must be found and spent. But taxpayers and subsidized producers and consumers alike are saying: "Don't balance the budget here."

Onrushing toward us are even more horrendously costly problems: the Savings and Loan crisis; environmental damage, past and ongoing; the polarizing priorities of "earth first" or "jobs first." Added to these is the challenge of the "peace threat." The Cold War and the "Evil Empire" theses have been extremely useful, even indispensable, to government in justifying the redistribution necessary to make up the economy's ever wider income and purchasing power shortfalls. Now the U.S. (as well as Western Europe and the Soviet Union, which have been playing the same game) can no longer use each other as bogies to frighten taxpayers into supporting the various forms of military boondoggle that have been used to prop up employment and profits in the domestic economy, and as an alternative "workfare" system for those unable to earn adequate market-generated incomes.

Unfortunately for our side, the Marxists had one thing right. There is a defect—an institutional bottleneck—which causes the market economy's growing sluggishness and ultimate breakdown. This bottleneck—Marx called it capitalism's fatal flaw—has been present in industrial economies from their inception.

The flaw can be traced to the father of market economics himself, Adam Smith, author of that extraordinary treatise, *The Wealth of Nations*, published in 1776, the date historians also assign to the start of the Industrial Revolution. Smith analyzed the economic order around him more or less as follows:

- Nature herself had invented the ideal economic system. She invented it simultaneously with the creation of man.
- Nature gave each human being a unique power: the power to deliberately produce goods and services. Human labor power was the original form of economic power.
- Nature's distribution of economic power was democratic: one person, one labor power.
- Nature clearly intended each human being to be self-supporting—neither slave nor parasite, but an autonomous producer.

- The purpose of production, Smith pointed out, is consumption by the producers themselves.

Economic power in Adam Smith's time was democratically diffused because every free human being owned his or her own labor power. Smith conceived the free-market economy to organize—on a national scale—the democratic economic plan Nature had devised for each individual. But Smith overlooked one thing. In the real economic world, people since the dawn of time had found that labor dependence has inherent limitations. To produce one's bread by the sweat of one's brow doomed men and women, other than slave owners, to unrelenting toil from dawn to dusk, from childhood to old age. And the reward was rarely more than bare subsistence.

Subsistence toil denied not only affluence but leisure—the prerequisite for education, the arts, culture—all that we call civilization. Man's body needs creature comforts but his mind and soul need leisure, because he is not only an animal but a spiritual being. The necessity for leisure was Aristotle's justification for the institution of slavery. However cruel and unjust, the slavery of some was necessary to enable others to create and enjoy civilization.

Thus the human race, long before 1776, had begun mobilizing a rebellion against its destiny of perpetual labor servitude. It invented tools, discovered fire, developed industrial processes. And right under Adam Smith's bespectacled nose, it was mounting its final onslaught against primordial toil and poverty. It was launching the Industrial Revolution—transferring the burden of production from the backs of men and animals to the forces of nature harnessed by the machine and other capital assets.

Smith did not notice that capital stock, as he called it, represented a new method for people to engage in production, one having the potential to liberate human beings from progressive increments of subsistence toil and compulsive poverty. It also enabled man, through capital asset ownership, to engage in production vicariously. The Industrial Revolution did not, and never will, eliminate the need for labor, for employment. But the labor worker becomes progressively less adequate as the revolution progresses and capital workers take over ever more of the burden of production and the rewards of earning capital-sourced income.

As an incomparable scholar and philosopher, Smith should have been familiar with Aristotle's speculation in Book I of his *Politics*. There was no alternative to slavery, Aristotle declared, unless, in some distant future, looms would weave and musical instruments play by themselves without the touch of human hands—in other words, until man managed to mount a successful industrial revolution. Then, said Aristotle, *everyone* would have mechanical slaves to perform subsistence toil on his behalf and in his stead. Capital instruments would be man's supplemental or surrogate producers.

In 1776, Aristotle's utopian vision was actually coming to pass. But Smith, blinkered by the labor theory of value, failed to see it. In Marshall McLuhan's famous phrase, he was looking into the future through the rear view mirror. Smith did not understand that capital gave its owner another way to make input into the production side of the market, just as he could through his labor. Consequently, Smith did not see that ownership of productive capital must become as widely distributed as labor power—and for precisely the same reasons that labor power is democratically distributed. Otherwise, Smith's free market formula would not work.

If one producer, through his privately-owned capital, produces and earns significantly more—even hundreds of times more—than he and his dependents can or will consume, then Say's Law—which holds that "supply" creates its own "demand"—does not work. Even the most lavish lifestyle has practical limits. Income not spent in the consumer markets is invested to accumulate even more excessive productive power for owners who cannot or will not devote it to consumption, as free-market logic assumes.

Nevertheless, Smith's basic insights into the dynamics of the free market were sound. The Industrial Revolution in no way invalidated the principles he identified. It did not change the rules. All it changed was the material and technological facts from which the concepts of working and earning were formulated. It did not change the rule that in order to earn income from production you must provide productive input. But it changed— as was the purpose of the Industrial Revolution—the nature of work from labor intensive to capital intensive. It invented a new kind of worker—the capital worker. To work today means to work increasingly with and through capital.

Therefore, universal capital ownership is not an option but, just as Aristotle foresaw, a necessity. People must earn incomes from capital ownership and use those incomes in the consumer markets if we are to avoid the political and economic ills that flow from wildly erratic and unreliable income distribution, or the need for coerced income redistribution from those who produce and earn to those who cannot because they are not capital-equipped to do so. Free-market logic equally commands every producer to be a consumer. The income generated by the free market must be spent to buy that market's current output. Otherwise we make depression inevitable.

Karl Marx, who shook the world with his *Communist Manifesto* in 1848, made the same mistake as Smith. But as he wrote three-quarters of a century later, he had less excuse for failing to see that not only was the Industrial Revolution changing the nature of work, that was its purpose. Marx's stirring descriptions of the gigantic, self-powered capital instruments of his day—Nasmyth's steam hammer was one—are unequalled in economic literature. How could Marx describe these autonomous machines in action, and record the human labor they superseded, yet still proclaim that only labor produces wealth?[6]

Marx thought that capital (improved land, structures, machines, processes and capital intangibles) was merely congealed labor power; that the value of capital represented theft by its owners—the capitalists—from helpless labor, and that the evils arising from privately concentrated economic power could only be corrected by abolishing private property in all producer goods and transferring ownership to the state. Today the world is awakening to the fact that Karl Marx's solution was not a solution at all, but a tragic mistake that destroyed both political freedom and the free market.

We do not think that Marx could have made such a disastrous error had he understood Aristotle's Utopian vision of automated production, in which every man was endowed with increased

---

6. See Louis Kelso, "Karl Marx: The Almost Capitalist," *American Bar Journal*, March, 1957, Vol. 43, No. 3.

economic power through the ownership of non-human slaves. But Western leaders are in no position to criticize either Smith or Marx for failing to understand the meaning of the Industrial Revolution, or its effect on work and income distribution, having also failed to understand it themselves.

There is more to Marx, however, than his erroneous views of private property in capital. There is another of his basic teachings called the "Marxian analysis." Marx greatly admired capital as the embodiment of technological change—the prize of the Industrial Revolution. He lauded the awesome power of capital to turn out vastly greater quantities of goods and services of higher quality than labor ever could do alone. But he realized that if only a few people acquire and own the economy's capital assets, they will be in a position to exploit and dominate the great non-capital owning, labor-dependent majority—the "proletarians." This reinforced his belief that private property in capital must be abolished. Marx believed that capital is such a good and necessary thing for society and humanity that it is wrong for only a few to monopolize its fruits. Can we really fault Marx on this? Would we want to?

Where does this leave us today?

Public ownership of capital, because it consolidates political and economic power, leads to the totalitarian state. But in private-property economies, capital ownership is concentrating faster than ever, while technological change makes capital ever more productive.

Smith said: every consumer a producer, and vice versa. But what neither Smith, nor Marx, nor the economists who have followed them have noticed is that capital workers are doing more and more of the producing.

So what do we do now? What should the faltering market economies do? What should the restructuring socialist economies do? What should the less-developed economies do?

Our answer is: adopt economic policies that acknowledge every citizen's right to become a capital worker as well as a labor worker. The means for doing this have already been invented and are described in detail in this book. The best known of them, the

Employee Stock Ownership Plan (ESOP)—is now in use by more than 11,000 corporations, including some of the largest.

More than 11 million ESOP employee participants are on their way to becoming capital workers. In the aggregate, they own over $50 billion of capital assets. But quite as important, ESOP companies are becoming more profitable and competitive. They are expanding, hiring more people, paying more taxes. It is not uncommon for participants in successful ESOP companies to retire with hundreds of thousands of dollars in company stock. Sold back to the ESOP, or retained for its earnings, this stock—assuming that the company remains significantly employee-owned so as to motivate new generations of labor workers—should provide comfort and security for them to the ends of their lives. Only through capital ownership can you engage in production and earn income when you leave the labor market because of age, illness, or business failure. Labor work is temporary; capital work provides lifetime employment.

Other financing methods embodying the ESOP's logic, and described here, can make capital workers of civil servants, teachers, nurses, artists, Social Security recipients and others outside the corporate sector. Like the ESOP, these techniques of business finance exploit the fact that, contrary to the conventional economic wisdom, people do not have to save to buy capital but can buy and pay for it out of its own earnings. You do not have to be a capital owner to be able to buy capital. Binary financing techniques open up capital ownership to those who are born without capital—most of the human race.

Any nation, industrialized or developing, can use these financing tools to speed up economic development; to free itself from foreign ownership; to both privatize and democratize the ownership of government-owned assets, and to build economic power into its own citizens and consumers so that neither they nor business and industry need government redistribution.

The national economic policies of all market economies—the United States, Canada, Great Britain, France, Germany, Japan, Mexico and all the rest—are out of date. They are oblivious to the cause and effects of the Industrial Revolution. They still assert, as a matter of policy, that everyone can live well on jobs alone. They imply just as positively that it makes no difference who owns the capital. They assume that industrial poverty can be cured through jobs and employment. They do not recognize that the human right to life, in an advanced industrial country, implies a right to earn a good living, and a right to earn a good living in a post-industrial economy implies the right to acquire capital out of its own income. Capital is a central part of the life support system of every post-industrial economy. Every family and every single individual needs to legitimately acquire and own a reasonable part of that life support system, so that the principles of free-market economics will work as Adam Smith envisioned in a preindustrial era.

Socialism has been discredited. Plutocracy is in the process of being discredited. Democratic capitalism has yet to be tried.

PART I

UNDERSTANDING ECONOMIC DEMOCRACY

CHAPTER 1

The Search for the Obvious

Great crises come when great new forces are at work
changing fundamental conditions, while powerful institutions and traditions still hold old systems intact.
—*William Graham Sumner, 1904*

Everywhere the realization is growing that something is wrong—
fundamentally and dangerously wrong—with the world's economic structure. People who want to work are finding it increasingly
difficult to earn a good living. Leaders in the Western industrial
democracies are tacitly abandoning their formal economic goal of
full employment, finding that the costs of creating it are unac-
ceptable.

Yet the historical tendency of the rich to grow richer and of the
poor to sink into dependency accelerates, while the middle class
loses ground or struggles to retain its tenuous foothold. Despite
awesome technological progress, the wondrous accomplishments
of science, engineering, agriculture, and public health, we seem
as stymied as ever by the wealth-poverty dichotomy that is turning neighborhoods, cities, nations, and the world itself into a battle-
ground of haves versus have-nots. Hopeless poverty, social alienation, and economic breakdown in a world that has all the physical,
technical, managerial, and engineering prerequisites for improving
the lives of millions attest to a crippling organizational malfunction
that prevents us from making full use of the powers we have developed. Many other apparently insoluable problems also point to
a structural defect: increasing economic dependence on arms production and sales, rising public and private debt, unmarketable
production surpluses in agriculture and manufacturing, the loss
of domestic and international markets to foreign competitors, and
the lack of an alternative to full-employment. The inability of our
leaders to solve these problems, or even contain them, is under-
mining confidence in democracy.

This book is concerned with root causes—the root cause of poverty and, more important, of affluence in the modern industrial world. It is concerned not only with economic helplessness and dependency, but also with economic power and independence. It investigates the source of personal and individual economic power, not to eliminate it, as the socialists have vowed to do, but to extend it beyond the rich to the traditionally disenfranchised poor and middle classes.

There is a wonderful word that has fallen into disuse as the economic conditions that gave it vitality have faded away—*competence*. Its oldest meaning, now obsolete, is sufficient supply, or a sufficiency. Its second meaning is property, or means sufficient to defray the costs of the necessities and conveniences of life: sufficiency without excess. The word further extends to the condition of possessing or enjoying such sufficiency—living in peace and competence, or the quality or state of being functionally adequate, or having sufficient knowledge, judgment, skill, or strength. "A man's first duty is to make a competence and to be independent," declared Andrew Carnegie.[1] In a prescient turn-of-the-century essay, Peter S. Grosscup, a U.S. Circuit Court of Appeals judge, pointed out, the "soul of republican America, as a civil government ordained to promote the welfare and happiness of its people" is not commercial greatness, territorial ambition, national power, or national wealth. Rather it is "individual opportunity— the opportunity and encouragement given to each individual to build up, by his own effort, and for himself and those dependent upon him, some measure of dominion and independence all his own."[2]

Having a competence is still the American economic ideal. The hope and chance of obtaining a competence is American economic opportunity. The right to have and hold a competence, once obtained, is a fundamental American right. Taken together, these conditions add up to economic happiness as the founding fathers understood it when they declared its pursuit on a parity with the right to life and liberty. Not enormous hoards of unusable and unspendable wealth, but competences and the recovery of individual hope and prospect—these are still the dream of the American people and the proper and necessary goals of U.S. economic policy.

For well over a century it has been obvious that our private-property, free-market, capitalist economy has a serious flaw.

Whether it is called the production-consumption gap, over-production, or under-consumption, its fundamental characteristic is the same: At any stage of economic growth or productive efficiency, the power available to produce goods and services outstrips the ability of the people with unsatisfied needs and wants to buy them. As Chief Sitting Bull told Annie Oakley, "The white man knows how to make everything, but he does not know how to distribute it."[3] Franklin D. Roosevelt made the same observation in his first inaugural address in the dark days of 1933: "Plenty is at our doorstep but a generous use of it languishes in the very sight of supply."

We must ask ourselves why western society has so long tolerated—indeed, remained officially blind to—obvious and repeatedly documented institutional defects. Why have we preferred myths to easily verifiable facts? For example, why are we still pretending to believe that labor is becoming more productive? That technology creates jobs? That we have ever achieved legitimate full employment in the United States in this century except when the nation is at war, recovering from war, or preparing for a new war? That full employment is a feasible, or even desirable, economic goal for people living in an industrial age?

The explanation is to be found in a simple but tenacious misconception about how goods and services are produced. The notion that labor is the only, or chief, factor is the keystone of conventional economic wisdom. Laissez-faire, Marxian, and Keynesian theoreticians all treat the physical things that are actually the chief producers of material goods and services in an industrial economy — tools, machines, structures, capital intangibles, and increasingly productive land—as if they were extensions of the worker himself (the hammer, an extension of the hand; the wheel, of the foot; the computer, of the brain) or as if they were natural resources functioning gratuitously like the sun to raise *labor* productiveness.

As long as we remain under the sway of fallacies like these, we are not concerned about *who* owns *what* capital (provided there is plenty of it) in our economy, nor do we realize that we have allowed the ownership of capital, and consequently the earning power of capital, to concentrate to the point of rendering the economy unworkable.

In the preindustrial past, when labor *was* the principal means of production, the labor theory of value was at least approximately true, and labor power was distributed democratically by nature—

one person equaled one unit of labor power. But with the invention of the spinning jenny, the Newcomen engine, the power loom, and hundreds of other capital instruments, the nonhuman factor began to dominate every aspect of production. Technology continues to transform the ways in which goods and services are produced, so that production is constantly becoming more capital intensive and less labor intensive. Today only human institutions can restore to men and women the autonomy they once had through their inherent labor power.

In the ancient and medieval worlds, toil had been only a means to an end: consumption and leisure. Now in an industrial age, as technological change systematically eliminates labor input into the production process—and with it, the only officially recognized way of participating in earning—we have perversely elevated toil from a practical necessity to a moral and social duty. Instead of toiling to live, people are increasingly living to toil. Under the laborcentric economic thought formalized in the earliest writings on economics, technology itself is presumed to create toil. The overwhelming evidence to the contrary is ignored, falsified, or rationalized away.

When a theory contrary to fact persists against all evidence, it must be drawing sustenance from a vital and powerful emotional source. The durability of the labor theory of value, the full-employment goal, and the institutions built upon them can be traced to the Puritan ethic, specifically to the idea that "if any would not work, neither should he eat." In essence, the Puritan ethic is a *production* ethic. It holds that people ought to be economically autonomous, that each consumer unit should earn the income equivalent of the goods and services it wishes to consume. This injunction is philosophically, economically, and morally sound. Experience shows that people hate being objects of charity just as much as they hate being victims of parasitism. Economic motivation requires that people both produce the goods and services they wish to consume and receive the income equivalent of their productive contribution.

In a preindustrial world, where labor provided most of the input into production, it was natural that production and toil became unconsciously identified. But what made sound practical and moral sense in a preindustrial economy becomes nonsense in an industrial one, not because the principle has changed but because the mechanics of production have changed. Anachronistic insistence that productive input is *labor* input solely and only, or even mainly, does not square with the facts. In an economy where people engage in production and earn income through their privately owned capital as well as their privately owned labor power, a laboristic interpretation of the Puritan ethic will not suffice, indeed, becomes more and more unjust. Conventional economic policies that exhort and inflict toil and self-denial no longer make sense in an age when technology has shifted most of the pains of production to the machine.

Institutional renewal and reform must begin with a reinterpretation of the Puritan ethic. If its moral message is not that people should toil for the sake of toil but that they should produce for the sake of consumption, then we must ask: How are all individuals to be adequately productive when a tiny minority (capital workers) produce a major share and the vast majority (labor workers), a minor share of total goods and services?

An updated Puritan ethic would acknowledge that individuals produce through their privately owned capital just as truly and legitimately as they do through their privately owned labor power. In the economic sense, the owner of an equity interest in an industrial corporation, a corporate farm, or other production facility can be immeasurably more productive than the most skilled and industrious preindustrial artisan. Production efficiency and product quality are what count, not the factor of production itself. Thus, the capital owner is not a parasite or a rentier but a worker—a *capital* worker. A distinction between labor work and capital work suggests the lines along which we could develop economic institutions capable of dealing with increasingly capital-intensive production, as our present institutions cannot.

There is another consideration. Economies can no longer solve their income distribution problem through full employment, even if this ever retreating and questionable goal were entirely achievable. When capital workers replace labor workers as the major suppliers of goods and services, labor employment alone becomes inadequate because labor's share of the income arising from production cannot provide the progressively better standard of living that technology is making possible. Labor produces subsistence at best. Capital can produce affluence. To enjoy affluence, all households must engage to an increasing extent in capital work. Under the facts of contemporary U.S. production, this would be so even if the entire population were fully employed in labor work.

As we will later show, the insufficiency of labor-based earnings to purchase increasingly capital-produced goods and services gave rise to labor laws and labor unions designed to coerce higher and higher prices for the same or reduced labor input. The myth of the "rising productivity" of labor is used to conceal the increasing productiveness of capital and the decreasing productiveness of labor, and to disguise income redistribution by making it seem morally acceptable.

Until we grasp the modern implications of the Puritan ethic, we will be unable to design an economic system that recognizes that there are *two* ways for individuals to engage in production and earn income. We will continue to misuse, misdirect, and waste technology in the name of full employment; concentrate capital ownership in the hands of those who already own more of it than they can or will use; and deny capital ownership to those who need to own it but cannot acquire it legitimately through traditional savings-based financing methods.

Leisure, not toil, and general affluence, not elitist wealth must be the goals of a rational and democratic industrial economy based on the need of every citizen to be a producer as well as a consumer. Moreover, once we recognize and articulate these goals, they are not difficult to achieve. One device, the Employee Stock Ownership Plan (ESOP), has already demonstrated how easy it is to make capital workers of corporate employees. Other financing devices that employ the same logic can accomplish the same transformation for public employees; for Social Security recipients; for artists, musicians, actors, and others not employed in the private or public sectors or suited to such employment; for customers of public utilities; and for home owners.

Since affluence is generally the product not of labor but of capital, the economy must be structured so that eventually all households produce an expanding proportion of their incomes through their privately owned capital and simultaneously generate enough purchasing power to consume the economy's output. The techniques of finance described in this book can legitimately connect households that own little or no capital with the productive power of capital instruments organized into appropriate operating entities. Conventional business finance has concentrated individual ownership of productive capital into the possession of the very few. The proprietary base is shrinking at an accelerating rate through mergers, acquisitions, and non-ESOP leveraged buyouts. Democratic financing methods, such as the Employee Stock Ownership Plan (ESOP), the Consumer Stock Ownership Plan (CSOP), the General Stock Ownership Plan (GSOP), and others, finance capital ownership for economically underpowered individuals at the same time that they finance corporate growth. They simultaneously create new capital owners and new productive power in ways that benefit everyone, including present stockholders.

New productive power is essential if everyone is to have some opportunity to become a capital worker. The limitations that prevent us from realizing our vast potential for general affluence are not physical but institutional. What is lacking are the implementing concepts—the logic diagram, the operating manual—for the private property, free-market economy that already splendidly serves the few, but that, by democratizing capitalism, we can expand to include and serve the many.

By updating the Puritan ethic to conform to the technological facts of life, we will renew not only our economy but also our political institutions in the spirit of the American ideal. American political institutions assume a citizenry of self-supporting families. They were never intended for a large and growing segment of poor and dependent people. In 1989 we will celebrate the 200th anniversary of the ratification of the U.S. Constitution. It is time that we do for economic power what the founding fathers did for political power: put it on the road to democracy.

NOTES

1. Andrew Carnegie, *The Empire of Business* (New York: Doubleday, Page & Co., 1902), p. 99.
2. Peter S. Grosscup, "How To Save the Corporation," *McClure's Magazine* 24, no. 4 (February 1905).
3. Dee Brown, *Bury My Heart at Wounded Knee: An Indian History of the American West* (New York: Holt, Rinehart & Winston, 1971), p. 427.

CHAPTER 2

Democracy's Missing Half

The unalienable rights of life, liberty, and the pursuit of happiness, the preservation of which was described in the Declaration of Independence as the primary reason why governments are instituted among men, belong to people and may not be taken away from people by any institution which man creates. This principle we must recognize as the cornerstone of our economic as well as of our political structure, for without it all freedom is endangered.

—*Joseph C. O'Mahoney*, 1941

For many Americans the definition of *democracy* begins "government by the people"—a political system that invests the individual citizens with sovereign power. Indeed, any dictionary corroborates that notion. But we often restrict our concept of democracy to its political aspect, unaware that democracy implies a broader system in which all citizens participate in the exercise of social power. Political democracy by itself is only half democracy because it allocates to citizens only half the totality of social power.

Let us define *social* power as power that can be wielded within a society by social means, that is, means free from brute force, undemocratic legal coercion, and fraud. That power is a composite of two kinds of power, each vital. One is *political* power: the power to make, interpret, administer, and enforce the laws. The other is *economic* power: the power to produce goods and services. If political democracy prescribes and requires that all citizens have the right to participate in the *political* process, then economic democracy confers on all individuals or families (consumer units) the right to participate in the *economic* process: the right to produce goods and services and to receive the income so earned.

Only one type of economic system is compatible with political democracy. That is the free market economy. It alone requires that every consumer unit participate in production to earn the income it spends for consumption, and it alone proportions the outtake (personal income) of each participant to his or her input into production. The American idea of democracy is an amalgam of political democracy—participation by all of its citizens in the process of government—and economic democracy—participation by each consumer unit in the production of goods and services to a degree sufficient to enable it to earn a good livelihood. Only where both halves of social power are democratized do we have *democracy*—a social structure designed to the human scale.

In countless seminars and lectures around the country, the authors have posed the question: "If you could have but one of the two forms of social power, which would you choose—political power or economic power?" We have yet to receive an answer other than the obvious. Everyone understands that the possessor of economic power can acquire political power. That is what Harrington meant in his famous dictum "Power follows property." To possess property, whether labor power or capital, is to possess a means of engaging in the production of goods and services and of earning income.

When the founding fathers recognized the rights to life, liberty, and the pursuit of happiness as inalienable human rights, they were affirming economic as well as political democracy. The two are inseparable and were understood to be so during the nation's first century. Universal suffrage "could not long exist in a community where there was a great inequality of property," declared Daniel Webster. "The freest government, if it could exist, would not be long acceptable, if the tendency of the laws were to create a rapid accumulation of property in few hands and to render the great mass of the population dependent and penniless. In such a case, the popular power must break in upon the rights of property, or else the influence of property must limit and control the exercise of popular power."[1]

The United States remained a working democracy from the time of its founding until around the close of the nineteenth century, when the American Industrial Revolution began in earnest. As technological advance amplified the productive power of capital, plutocratic finance channeled its ownership into fewer and fewer hands. The decline of economic democracy was obscured by the simultaneous rise of political democracy, which was increasingly accepted as the only significant kind of democracy. Millions of immigrants, escaping from homelands historically ruled by auto-cratic wealth, had no experience with either political or economic power. Nor could the latter-day newcomers hope for a property stake on the western frontier.

America's founding fathers themselves fixed their attention on political power, which they wanted to wrest from Great Britain in order to more fully exploit and enjoy the economic power they had already obtained thanks to their early arrival, fortunate connec-tions, and the virgin opportunities of a largely uninhabited conti-nent. The authors of the Constitution, even more than those of the Declaration of Independence, fully understood that economic power and political power were indivisible. Property was their summum bonum, as precious as life or liberty. To uphold the rights to acquire and protect property, government was ordained. These men did not believe that *equality* of property was a necessary or even desirable coefficient of political equality. Implicit in their ar-guments and discussions, however, is the understanding that a measure of economic power is prerequisite to a responsible use of political power. These men believed that people who had no prop-erty or hope of acquiring property would have only one use for the political franchise: to vote themselves the property of others.

Again and again this danger was emphasized at the Constitu-tional Convention. In support of property qualifications for voters James Madison warned the convention delegates: "An increase of population will of necessity increase the proportion of those who will labor under all the hardships of life and secretly sigh for a more equal distribution of its blessings. These may in time out-number those who are placed above the feelings of indigence. Ac-cording to the equal laws of suffrage, the power will slide into the hands of the former."[2]

The delegates defeated property qualifications and left voting rights to the states not so much because these delegates advocated Jeffersonian democracy as for the reason that they represented dif-ferent economic and sectional interests and thus could not agree on which property qualifications to impose. Why, then, did such a conservative and politically sophisticated elite introduce the revo-lutionary doctrine of political equality? Charles Beard attributes their action to America's unique economic circumstances. "There was no established clergy here. There was no titled aristocracy. There was no such proletariat as formed the 'mob' of Paris. Land was the chief form of property and its wide distribution among the whites (leaving the slaves out of account) brought about in fact a considerable economic equality to correspond to the theory of political equality."[3] But there was an additional circumstance that exerted perhaps even more influence on the shape of America's political institutions. This was the dominant productive importance of labor, which, in tandem with plentiful and cheap land, gave uncapitalized citizens unprecedented economic power.

Political democracy, then, was introduced into a natural economic democracy. Indeed, the economic democracy extant at the nation's birth was considerably more solid and extensive than the political democracy superimposed upon it. "All men are created equal" disregarded large categories of the populace—women, native Americans, slaves, unpropertied men. Moreover, despite the founding fathers' devotion to property rights, the most fundamental of these—the right of every individual to own totally his or her own labor power—was only selectively respected. The South considered slavery an economic necessity. Several signers of the Declaration of Independence were slaveowners, most notably Thomas Jefferson. Bonded servants, often disguised as apprentices, were a colonial institution. Full democratization of economic power would have demanded the abolition of both voluntary and involuntary servitude throughout the new nation. Our nation's founders, however, were political realists. Supporters of the plutocracy inherited from Great Britain, represented by Alexander Hamilton, were as numerous and influential as supporters of democracy. A flawed and limited democracy was not only better than none, it was perhaps what a majority of the founding fathers themselves preferred. The prevailing colonial economic democracy was, in a sense, an accident. It was the result of the high productiveness of labor in a low-technology economy, the plentifulness of cheap land, and the enormous need for labor to make the land productive. All three of these conditions were temporary.

The "Divine Right" of the Rich

The agrarian and preindustrial American economy began with a tiny capital-owning class—among them the founding fathers and their friends. These men and their families acquired ownership of the privately owned and much of the publicly owned land capital within and beyond the original thirteen colonies. They were eager to sever colonial ties with Great Britain, not just to gain political freedom, but to avoid having to share their new-found and potentially enormous wealth with the Old World aristocracy.

By the time the Industrial Revolution reached American shores, about 1815, the few original capitalists—those who had gained their wealth by grants, charters, and land purchases from the English and European crowns—were economically entrenched, having used their landed collateral and acquisitive expertise to supersede the nascent loyalist plutocracy of explorers, merchants, and traders. Now two familiar phenomena came to their aid. First was technology itself. As historian Arnold Toynbee reminds us, the Industrial Revolution "is a revolutionary change in the nature of the agent who [sic] does the world's work. It is a replacement of people by machinery."[4] This change primarily and directly benefits capital owners—those who own the land, structures, machines, and capital intangibles. Technological changes that raise the productiveness of labor, such as switching from cottage industry to factory production, job rationalization, and specialization, do not significantly or reliably raise the value of labor; more frequently these changes reduce the demand for labor and thus reduce its value.

The other phenomenon that empowered America's original capitalists was conventional savings-based finance. Access to capital credit was, as it remains today, generally available only to those who were already well capitalized. Thanks to conventional finance, initially entrenched land ownership gave the colonial aristocracy almost the same exclusivity of rights over the development of industrial capital that the divine-right doctrine had earlier conferred on preindustrial kings and nobility. Thus the newly created class of American hereditary rich began to grow richer, while the newly arrived toiling masses, for the most part, remained poor and capitalless.

Opportunities, of course, did exist for some new arrivals to gain a foothold among the American elite. Those who had, or quickly acquired and exploited, the technical and managerial know-how demanded by the burgeoning enterprises of the new nation could reach the top. Andrew Carnegie, himself an upstart Scottish immigrant, was an obsessive cutter of labor costs. Nevertheless, he did not hesitate to make shareholders of those managers whom he considered indispensable and whom he could not retain at a lesser price. The practice of law and the holdings of judgeships also offered special opportunities to ambitious young men to acquire capital estates. Further, there were the modest but significant opportunities presented by the western frontier, before and after the Homestead laws first enacted in 1862, and by government sale of public lands to settlers, miners, and railroad and canal entrepreneurs for token payments.

But by the end of the nineteenth century the American frontier was virtually closed. Land not occupied had been skillfully maneuvered into ownership of the territories and the states. Thus warehoused, this landed capital could later be exploited by the already rich and their corporations. Thus, again excepting the few who in every age are gifted with luck or genius, capital ownership in the American economy evolved from the concentrated land holdings created initially through powers emanating from the notion of the divine right of kings to the concentration of most nonresidential capital ownership—landed, industrial, and service enterprise—in the top 5 percent of wealthholders and their institutions today.[5] Indeed, a study of the domestic market for luxury goods published in 1985 by Grey Advertising stated:

All things considered, it seems unlikely that as much as 5 percent of the population has the financial wherewithal to qualify for even comparative affluence. As for absolute affluence, the population is even smaller—limited to those sparsely inhabited zones where $75,000 starts to look like small change.

According to the Federal Reserve Board, the 2 percent of U.S. families who earn $100,000 or more a year own 20 percent of all residential property, 30 percent of all liquid assets, 33 percent of all business property, 39 percent of all bonds, 50 percent of all stocks and 71 percent of all tax-free financial holdings.[6]

Will and Ariel Durant concluded in *The Lessons of History:* "The relative equality of Americans before 1776 has been overwhelmed by a thousand forms of physical, mental, and economic differentiation, so that the gap between the wealthiest and the poorest is now greater than at any time since Imperial plutocratic Rome."[7]

Some Consequences of Technological Advance

We owe this inequality primarily to the fact that technological advance, with rare exceptions, raises the productiveness of capital instruments, which primarily benefits their owners. Advance does not generally make labor, as such, more productive. In fact, the opposite is true. As capital work supersedes labor work, the demand for labor work diminishes, and the value of labor tends to fall. Free-market forces no longer establish the "value" of labor. Instead, the price of labor is artificially elevated by government through minimum wage legislation, overtime laws, and collective bargaining legislation or by government employment and government subsidization of private employment solely to increase consumer income.

It is often said that the skills required to enable workers to use modern technology are higher skills that command higher competitive prices simply because a longer formal education is required to qualify such persons for these skills. These alleged "higher" skills are really only *different* skills and generally involve less overall knowledge, less effort, less risk, and less learning time than the skills they displaced. For example, the modern jet pilot requires less skill than the original bush pilot, even though he navigates with far more sophisticated and expensive capital instruments. A modern production line worker requires vastly less skill than the craftsman who preceded him in the marketplace; he may be needed only to check the behavior of robots. The function of human intellect in the economic world is to push the burden of production off labor and onto capital workers with their machines, that is, to "save work."

One of the earliest observers of the impact of technological change on the character of democracy in America was Peter Grosscup, a judge of the United States Circuit Court for the Sixth Circuit. Born in 1852 in Ohio, Judge Grosscup was himself a product of the labor-intensive economic democracy of the frontier.

A generation ago, the artisans of the country lived in the country towns. In the country towns were made the shoes we wore, the wagons and carriages, the stoves, the saddlery we used—all the appliances of life; and over the door of each shop hung the sign of the proprietor within. A generation ago, the farm work was done by men living on the farms.

All this is now changed. Nearly one-half of the population of the United States—twelve million active workers, supporting as dependents twenty-four million more—are now connected with the mechanical trades. The men who, in the time of which I have just spoken, with their own hands did the planting and cultivating and harvesting, are now in the manufacturing centers, making the machines that plant and cultivate and harvest. The artisan proprietors in the towns have been succeeded by artisan employees in the great factories. The whole scene of industrial activity has been shifted from town and country to the cities; from the numerous small dominions exercised by individuals, to colossal corporate dominions.[8]

The relative economic democracy of America's first century resulted from the diminutive importance of capital, other than land, and the overwhelming importance of labor. Nearly all of the value of economic input came from labor in colonial days. Redistribution of earned income, except for the small efforts of churches and benevolent associations, was unknown. People were economically self-sufficient, although the standard of living was, of course, low. Even a wealthy landowner like George Washington enjoyed very modest possessions and comforts. Then as now, labor produced — at best — subsistence. It is capital — particularly industrial capital — that produces affluence.

For all practical purposes, economic power in an agrarian economy was democratically distributed by nature herself: One man or one woman equaled one unit of labor power. The practice of slavery, of course, concentrated many labor powers into the hands of the slaveowner and his family. But in an agrarian economy, where land is the overwhelmingly dominant form of capital, free men and women represent in their own persons the democratic distribution of economic power. Raw land could not be made economically valuable without enormous applications of hard and sustained labor. Many different kinds of labor inputs were required whether the land was to be used for farming, mining, timber raising, or as a building site. Consequently, the founding fathers rightly assumed that economic democracy existed in 1776, even though early-comers like themselves had already claimed the best lands along the eastern seaboard and in the South. Vastly greater quantities of land were available in the American continent for those industrious and ambitious enough to discover and claim it. Thus for generations the westward-moving frontier revitalized economic democracy, even while both were in the process of vanishing.

Without an understanding of the composite nature of social power, it was inevitable that democracy in the United States would be destroyed by advancing industrialization and plutocratic finance.

The economy changed from labor intensive to capital intensive. Population increased. The reserves of land available to individuals expired, while the relative productive importance of fabricated capital—machines, structures, and processes—grew in relation to that of land.[9] By 1850 industrial capital had outstripped agricultural capital in value. But the labor-dependent many had no means, or grossly inadequate means, for attaining through capital ownership the economic power they were losing to "progress." This was the phenomenon Judge Grosscup observed and found so ominous for America's future.

Industrialization made the business corporation the dominant vehicle of modern American life—in Judge Grosscup's metaphor, it became the gravitational force of an industrial system, holding all of its activities in orbit. This switch from individual to corporate ownership would have no great significance, thought Judge Grosscup, "if the corporation were only this age's new way of unifying, massing, individual ownerships—leaving the people of the country, generally, though under this new form, the ultimate real owners." But this was not what was coming to pass. The corporation's effect was "to drive the bulk of our people, other than farmers, out of property ownership; and. . .to keep them out." Private property, democratically distributed, was the foundation on which the American Republic and the American character were built. To restore her fast vanishing democracy, America had to learn how to make this new form of capital ownership a workable agent toward "repeopleizing the proprietorship of the country's industries," just as earlier the Homestead and Preemption laws had "peopleized the proprietorship of the public domain."[10]

A Democratic Capitalist Economy

A *democratic capitalist economy* is a private-property, free-market economy in which goods and services are produced through the voluntary and universal cooperation of concurrent labor workers and capital workers under a politically democratic government. Distribution of the proceeds of production is based upon the private property rights of labor workers in their labor power and capital workers in their capital, the size of their distributive shares being determined by the extent of their labor or capital input as evaluated through the mechanism of free competition. Each household's ability to produce enough income to enjoy its self-chosen lifestyle obviously hinges on the adequacy of its power to make productive input. As the production of goods and services changes from labor intensive to capital intensive, it is clear that the way in which every household participates in production and earns income must similarly change from labor to capital intensive. The workability of the economy—the continued democratization of its economic power and the continuous economic autonomy of its consumers—requires that capital ownership of undercapitalized consumers be progressively enlarged. This is the only alternative to income redistribution for providing consumer demand. Economic health also requires vigilance in preventing families from accumulating more capital-earning power than they can or wish to spend on their own consumption.

A market economy is essentially a double-entry bookkeeping system based on the fact that each household in market economies has a double role of consumer and producer. Costs paid for production on one side of the ledger become personal incomes earned for consumption on the other. The economy itself is a vital organism engaged primarily in the current production of consumer goods and services for current consumption.[11] Any sustained accumulation of capital-produced income in excess of that actually used to pay for things consumed will inevitably be channeled into the ownership of progressively greater capital-earning power. At the time when such capital-earning power exceeds the demands of a household's consumer lifestyle, it becomes sterilized and unusable, so far as the economy is concerned; it also actively violates the common law of individual property rights.

Clearly, the U.S. economy is not at present a private-property, democratic-capitalist, free-market economy, nor is any other economy on earth. We have all the essential ingredients. What is missing? Primarily a theory of democratic capitalism to show how these ingredients combine into a continuously functioning and growing system, along with the financing methods to implement this concept in ways wholly compatible with the U.S. Constitution and the protection of private property. Only a sound political-economic concept that is implemented by appropriate institutions will perpetuate democracy in the industrial world.

Plutocratic capitalism, despite its inefficiency and cost in human suffering and its affront to the constitutional rights of all citizens, has taught us some valuable lessons. It has helped us develop virtually all the institutional components required by a private-property, democratic-capitalist, free-market economic system. But it has not taught us how to use those components to achieve our own personal and social goals—individual political and economic freedom, general affluence, leisure, and peace; in short, the true democracy our nation pledged itself to build and uphold. Blinded by the myths and ideologies of the past, we have not yet correctly perceived the implications of the Industrial Revolution for free-market economies. Thus we have overlooked the first step on the road to industrial-age democracy.

The theory of democratic capitalism fills this void. With it, we can build an economy of universally productive individuals and households. We can, in time, inoculate people against poverty. Legitimately and constitutionally we can raise the earning power of the underproductive and prevent the sterilization of excess capital productive power accumulated by those who will not and cannot use it for their own consumption. We can tame, if not wholly eliminate, the business cycle in the American economy. We can plan and deliberately effect economic health, both for the national economy and for each consumer unit within it. We can indeed demonstrate for the world how to produce goods and services in such a way as eventually to make all consumers economically autonomous, as they were under nature's original economic plan for preindustrial humanity.

NOTES

1. Charles A. Beard, *The Economic Basis of Politics* (New York: Vintage Books, 1957), p. 39.
2. Ibid., p. 142.
3. Ibid., p. 65.
4. Arnold Toynbee, *The State Journal* (East Lansing, Michigan), April 18, 1971, "Views on the News" section.
5. While quantitative studies indicate there are some 42 million shareholders in the United States, qualitative studies show virtually all capital ownership of every form except family residences to be in the top 5 percent of consumer units. As to indirect ownership through financial intermediaries such as insurance companies, pension funds, and mutual funds, these kinds of investments are

almost never acquired on a self-liquidating basis. In other words, they do not provide an opportunity for an individual to buy capital and to pay for it out of his or her own income, derived from the newly acquired capital, so they do not make a net increase in the buyer's earning power and standard of living. Except where such savings are made by the rich and their corporations, they represent a reduced present standard of living and the storing of purchasing power, subject to the effects of inflation, for future use. In our advanced industrial economy it is rare indeed, except where a well-designed ESOP is involved, for anyone to acquire through personal saving a capital holding that would yield a viable income. See Marshall E. Blume, Jean Crockett, and Irwin Friend, *Stock Ownership in the United States: Characteristics and Trends*, Survey of Current Business, U.S. Department of Commerce, Bureau of Economic Analysis, vol. 54, no. 11, pp. 16–40; "Survey of Consumer Finances, 1983," *Federal Reserve Bulletin* 70, no. 9 (September 1984): 679–92; "Survey of Consumer Finances, 1983: A Second Report," *Federal Reserve Bulletin* 70, no. 12 (December 1984): 857–68; Robert J. Lampman, *The Share of Top Wealth-Holders in National Wealth, 1922–1956* (Princeton: Princeton University Press, 1962), pp. 23, 108, 195; Russell B. Long, "Employee Stock Ownership Plans: Spreading the Wealth to the Average American Worker," *The American University Law Review* 26, no. 3 (Spring 1977): 515; McClaughry Associates, Inc., *Expanded Ownership* (Fond du Lac, Wisc.: The Sabre Foundation, 1971), pp. 101–98; "Financial Characteristics of High-Income Families," *Federal Reserve Bulletin* 72, no. 3 (March 1986).

6. *Grey Matter*, "Auditing American Affluence: Are We Really Getting Richer?" (New York: Grey Advertising, 1985), pp. 5–6.

7. Will Durant and Ariel Durant, *The Lessons of History* (New York: Simon and Shuster, 1968), p. 55.

8. Peter S. Grosscup, "How To Save the Corporation," *McClure's Magazine* 24, no. 4 (February 1905).

9. There are no known limitations to the amount of fabricated capital that can be created, so long as effective consumer demand—physical demand matched with consumer purchasing power—remains unsatisfied.

10. Grosscup, "How To Save the Corporation."

11. Producer goods—capital assets intended to facilitate the production of consumer goods and services—do not follow free-market principles of supply and demand but rather are governed, in a free democratic society like that established by the U.S. Constitution, by the theory of capitalism. That theory is simultaneously simple and complex. It will be discussed in Chapter 3.

CHAPTER 3

The Concept of
Democratic Capitalism

Every man has a right to life; and this means that he also
has the right to make a comfortable living. He may by
sloth or crime decline to exercise that right; but it may
not be denied him.
— *Franklin D. Roosevelt,* 1932

Like the fact that there are two ways to participate in production
and to earn income in a free-market, industrial economy, the theory
of democratic capitalism is easy to state but exceedingly difficult for
our myth-conditioned minds to comprehend. It consists of three
precepts: (1) the property principle, (2) the participation principle,
and (3) the limitation principle. Considered alone, each precept is
invalid; only when all three are simultaneously and equally recognized in practice may democratic capitalism be said to exist or economic justice to prevail. Think of them as the legs of the democratic
capitalist tripod. If one leg is eliminated, the structure falls; if one
leg is lengthened or shortened without corresponding alterations
in the other two, the structure loses its balance and topples.

Property

In law and economics, the term *property* identifies the ownership
by a person of a specific productive asset. It refers to a composite of
rights. Property in producer goods includes, most importantly, the
right to receive all that is produced by the thing owned, whether
through capital or one's own labor power. To the degree that this
right is curtailed, one's property in the thing owned is diminished
or destroyed.

The bundle of rights constituting property is not absolute. It does not include the right to use the thing owned so as to injure the life, liberty, or property of another or to use the thing owned in a way that impairs the general welfare. These limitations are explicit in the American common law. Property is a fundamental and inalienable human right. It is the keystone of economic justice and of economic participation. It is thus essential to the concept of democratic capitalism.

Participation

The principle of participation is inherent in the right to life—the first inalienable right affirmed in the Declaration of Independence. Without the right to produce the means of sustaining life, neither the right to life nor the right to liberty nor the right to pursue one's economic happiness can be exercised in practice.

Capital, the chief factor of production in an industrial economy, is critical even in a primitive society since production is impossible without land and natural resources. Only participation through capital ownership liberates humankind from its hereditary labor servitude and provides people, depending on the state of technology, a measure of political and economic autonomy and leisure to devote to the work of civilization.

The logic of free-market economics leaves no doubt that the only economically legitimate way to earn income is to participate in production. This means that the breadwinners for each family must earn the income for that family. Welfare, whatever its form, is a charitable or political expedient; it does not involve the exercise of the right to be productive, a right implicitly and explicitly assured to every citizen by the U.S. Constitution.

Limitation

Philosophically, the principle of limitation is based on a distinction between means and ends. Capital-produced income is a means when it provides its owner with the consumer income necessary to enable his or her household to enjoy its chosen mode of life. Ownership of sufficient wealth to satisfy that requirement is both legitimate and desirable. Accumulation of more capital than is required to meet the owner's consumption needs and wants and to free him or her from subsistence toil is, however, quite a different matter. Wealth-getting then is treated as an end in itself. It violates the right of others to be adequately capitalized. It also violates the limitations on the use of property that are essential parts of the common law of property.

In a primitive economy, where the active factor of production—labor power—was evenly distributed and land was plentiful, or in any event uncooperative without massive labor input, there was no way to concentrate the power to produce income and accumulate wealth except by monopolizing land or by appropriating the wealth of others through theft or fraud or enslavement. In the totalitarian slave societies of the past, genuine affluence was enjoyed only by the ruling classes. Affluence depended, with rare exceptions, on being born into the class that owned super-viable holdings of land and slaves. The monopolization of land and labor power, through slavery, were the chief sources of exploitation, misery, and injustice in that world. As long as man's tools remained simple and relatively accessible, concentrated ownership of fabricated capital was not an insuperable economic problem. But when fabricated capital began to supplement land and simple, handmade tools were replaced by ever more complex, powerful, sophisticated, and costly devices, concentrated ownership by a few deprived others—the vast majority—of their right to acquire, own, and protect property and also of their right to earn their livelihoods by means that both raise their earning power and legitimately liberate them to some degree from toil.

One aspect of the income distribution problem arises from the simple fact that the rich are often so rich that they cannot consume what their capital produces. The excess income yield of their holdings thus is rendered barren and sterile—both to the rich, who have reached and surpassed the limits of their consumer capacity or desires, and to the poor, who, because of the input-outtake or double-entry bookkeeping nature of a free-market economy, are thereby prevented from earning the standard of living they would freely choose.

This is the essence of social injustice. It denies the capitalless majority of citizens their right to be productive—a right dependent in our industrial age upon effective opportunity to acquire, own, and protect capital. It denies them equal protection of the laws, which would give them equal access to the freedom and independence that capital ownership provides and enhances.

It follows that if every household must own *enough* capital, no household can or should own *too much* because the aggregate of what is produced equals the aggregate power to consume generated by production. If the few produce what must be consumed by the many, the many are deprived of their power to produce for themselves and either become wards of charity or die of privation. The condition of too much is reached when a household or consumer unit's capital holdings produce more income than its members wish to spend and in fact do spend on consumption to maintain their preferred and habitual mode of life. This limit is not absolute or arbitrary, but is related to individual consumption patterns, freely chosen by the individuals concerned, and to the prevailing state of technology.

People alive today have suffered so greatly from the defects of capitalism as it has been practiced that most will have difficulty in accepting the principle of limitation until they have been convinced that the restoration of economic democracy has eliminated inflation and the most erratic gyrations of the business cycle. Generations have suffered periodic economic ruin or the threat of ruin. Anticipated poverty shadows even the lives of middle-class people who, lacking adequate capital ownership, live with the haunting possibility of losing what they have gained. Millions identify with professor and author Irving Howe, who, discussing the scars left on him by the Great Depression, wryly told *Business Week*: "I don't know how much money I need to feel secure, but clearly it's more than I will ever have."[1] Such fears and anxieties are deep seated, widespread, and well founded for people living in a one-factor economy. Our implementation of the principle of limitation, initially and for those presently alive, should allow latitude for rainy day protection in the form of capital holdings somewhat larger than justified by current and anticipated consumption projections.

When a democratized capitalist economy begins to earn the people's confidence, and when it is again understood, as it was in ages schooled by Aristotle and Aquinas, that wealth is not an end in itself but a means to an end—namely, to a good life and a society that encourages the cultivation of virtue and the advancement of civilization—the principle of limitation will be increasingly accepted. We should keep in mind that the principle of limitation is by no means new; it is a basic social idea that has found expression in all ages. It is the moral of Aesop's fable of the dog in the manger. It is the impetus behind the universal religious command that the rich treat the poor in a charitable manner. Indeed, it is an idea sanctioned by all religions, and central to both Christianity[2] and Judaism.[3] It conditions our thinking about the concentrated ownership of wealth in times past and present.

The sole purpose of economic activity in a free-market, private-property economy is the production of goods and services for human consumption and enjoyment *by the producers*. This elemental fact is itself a natural principle of limitation: It tells us that we should not produce more than we desire to use for ourselves and our dependents. This is the essence of the idea of economy. It is likewise the essence of the idea of property. Not only does property convey the aggregate rights of control, including the right to the entire yield of the thing owned, but as social beings, individuals are subject to the limitation that they may not use their property in such a way as to injure the person or property of another.

Finally, natural law through death itself imposes the ultimate principle of limitation. Property ceases at death. An individual's identity, person, *proper* self (from whence comes the word *property*) ends at death. The right to make gifts of one's capital and assets ceases at death. Transfers of property at death, either through institutions or by will, including their taxation, belong to the domain of positive law and public policy. This is also true of limitations on transfers, such as those to charitable foundations, intended to circumvent laws regulating testamentary gifts. Thus the principle of limitation extends to, and countermands, all stratagems to subvert it.

The legal implementation of the principle of limitation—its application to every situation—is, of course, a task for federal and state legislatures. No specific legislation regulating a capitalist economy is more critical than this.

What constitutes a viable capital estate? How large should it be? In a free society that is a question for each household to decide for itself, subject to the power of government to enforce the limitation set forth in the common law of property. But the logic to which Congress must resort, both under the concept of economic justice and under the philosophy behind the Declaration ot Independence and the Constitution, is the equal right of each consumer unit to the opportunity to produce under competitive conditions the income necessary to enjoy the standard of living it reasonably chooses for itself. "Reasonably" refers to the physical capacity of the economy. If its physical capacity is smaller than the aggregate of chosen living standards—a condition that modern technology makes highly unlikely—then Congress must, with equal protection to each, define a lower limit of viability that will prevent any capital-owning family from injuring anyone else's person or property or the public welfare. Social policy concerning family size will here become an essential political consideration.

Strict observance of the principle of limitation is critical for other reasons as well. The widespread use of welfare, which technological advance makes unavoidable under our present one-factor economic policy, destroys the stability of any monetary system. The chaos unleashed by unstable money represses the production of goods and services, economic growth, and the increase of toil-free time.

All personal labor income should be exempt from the principle of limitation. If an Elvis Presley can, primarily through his labor power, earn $100 million, or a John Lennon can earn $230 million,[4] a policy of protecting property in the fruits of personal labor, of granting utmost personal freedom and encouraging personal creativity, would suggest a policy of noninterference by government. Excessive productive and purchasing power, however, should not be used for capital investments that violate the principle of limitation. The exceptional earner might make personal gifts of his excess to friends, relatives, employees, or others who lack viable capital estates.

Similarly, building or improving one's residence or surroundings, or creating goods and performing services through one's own craftsmanship, skills, and talents, should not be considered as violations of the principle of limitation. These are creative contributions to the quality of life for all. Craftsmanship is unique to labor; we should encourage exercising it for its intrinsic satisfaction and aesthetic value.

There is a logical parallel here with labor work. Employment of labor is also a means to an end: consumer income. Where employment is necessary to produce income to sustain a chosen living standard, it is honorable. The use of human talents and time to produce income or to produce goods or services that can be effectively produced by capital under the prevailing state of technology, however, is questionable; it makes a goal of toil and subverts leisure. There is neither honor nor dignity in toil expended to produce goods or services that capital instruments can produce just as well or better. In the ordering of human affairs, at least at this stage of the Industrial Revolution, capital is the *primary* and labor the *secondary* factor of production.

How can the principle of limitation be enforced in a society like ours, where unlimited accumulations have not only been permitted but encouraged, admired, and heralded as heroic achievements? Understanding the logical structure of the private-property economy is the first step. Much of the greed problem will be solved by institutional reforms that (1) cause capital ownership to grow in those consumer units that are economically underpowered and (2) cause the wages of capital to be paid out as fully as the wages of labor. In other words, the principles of property and of participation automatically reinforce the principle of limitation.

The institutional conclusion we should draw from the principle of limitation is that both the political and economic health of a democratic-capitalist, free-market economy depend on redesigning and administering its institutions so that the ownership of capital grows in the right places and, conversely, so that it does not grow in the wrong places. Ownership must grow in every consumer unit to make that unit economically autonomous. It must not grow in any consumer unit to an extent that endangers democratic capitalism by creating unused capital holdings.

The theory of democratic capitalism makes a clear distinction between intolerable greed and the ownership of just enough capital — enough to constitute a competence. Its guidelines are firm and clear. When one has acquired sufficient capital-sourced earning power to satisfy one's consumer needs and wants, sufficient to reasonably provide the living one wishes to enjoy, one has *enough* capital-oriented earning power. To then acquire more earning power, through more capital ownership, is to violate the principle of limitation that is an essential element in the franchise to acquire and own capital in the first place.

NOTES

1. *Business Week*, 50th Anniversary Issue (September 3, 1979): 50.
2. See Dom Virgil Michel, *St. Thomas and Today: Comments on the Economic Views of Aquinas* (St. Paul, Minn.: Wanderer Printing Co., 1936).

3. See the eight degrees of charity enumerated by the twelfth-century philosopher Moses Maimonides, translated from *Matnot Aniyim* 10, 7, in *The Union Prayerbook for Jewish Worship, Part II* (New York: The Central Council of Jewish Rabbis, 1962), pp. 117–18.
4. *The Economist*, December 31, 1980.

CHAPTER 4

Say's Law Reconsidered

Consumption is the sole end and purpose of all production; and the interest of the producer ought to be attended
to only so far as it may be necessary for promoting that
of the consumer. The maxim is so perfectly self-evident
that it would be absurd to attempt to prove it. But in the
mercantile system the interest of the consumer is almost
constantly sacrificed to that of the producer; and it seems
to consider production, and not consumption, as the ultimate end and object of all industry and commerce.
—*Adam Smith, 1770*

The disassociation of production and consumption, already a problem at the time of Adam Smith, has been carried to its most ir-
rational extreme in the United States economy. Americans have
forgotten that there is only one sane reason for producing goods
and services—so that we, the producers, can use them to enhance
our daily lives. In dropping the object of consumption from our
economic equation, and substituting employment as the goal for
the capitalless many and the accumulation of unlimited economic
productive power for the capital-owning few, we not only violate
the principles of equal economic opportunity and equal protection
of the laws, but we also abuse the operational logic of a market
economy.

The private-property, free-market economy, so long as there is
reasonable equality of economic opportunity, is a self-regulating
mechanism—a feedback mechanism in the terminology of the systems engineer. It is illustrated in Figure 4–1.

The logic illustrated by Figure 4–1 is derived from the principle
articulated by French political economist Jean Baptiste Say. Economists promptly named this discovery "Say's Law of Markets" and
compressed its message into an aphorism: "Supply creates its own
demand." The figure shows a balance in which equilibrium exists

Figure 4–1. Say's Law as Applied to a National Economy.

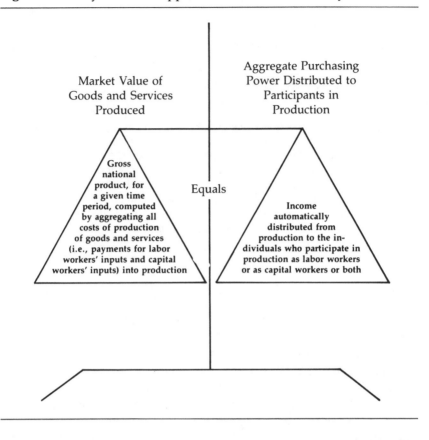

Market Value of Goods and Services Produced

Aggregate Purchasing Power Distributed to Participants in Production

Gross national product, for a given time period, computed by aggregating all costs of production of goods and services (i.e., payments for labor workers' inputs and capital workers' inputs) into production

Equals

Income automatically distributed from production to the individuals who participate in production as labor workers or as capital workers or both

only when both pans weigh the same during a specific period of time such as a calendar or fiscal year. The left pan represents the value of the net goods and services produced, or the gross national product, computed by adding together all costs of production: the payments to all capital workers and labor workers at every stage and in every area of production; the costs of all resources, materials, and supplies; all transportation and administration costs; and the costs of government paid through taxes. The right pan aggregates the costs incurred by producers in purchasing the inputs represented by the left pan.

Say's Law assumes, at minimum, the degree of equality of economic opportunity that prevailed in preindustrial society. Then, people differed in physical strength, endurance, intelligence, talents, and skill, and these variations were reflected in each family's subsistence-earning power. Within the family, wide disparities in ability were tolerated and accommodated. The least able members depended on the more able. Compassion, affection, and self-interest enforced the socialistic principle of distribution: from each according to ability, to each according to need. But when technology evolved to the Industrial Revolution and beyond, the primitive equality of preindustrial economic opportunity was destroyed. Creating economic opportunities for all households appropriate to the new industrial condition became the task and responsibility of nature's surrogate, the state.

In the industrial world, it is human institutions, authorized and presided over by the state, that must make the capital-based power to produce accessible to all consumers. The United States is fortunate that its founding fathers sensed the direction in which a free society must move. The economic guidelines they set forth in the Declaration of Independence and the Constitution prepare the way for democracy to flourish, even at advanced stages of technological evolution, if only we are vigilant in applying the fundamental principles to the changing industrial facts of life.

The state must aggressively fulfill its tutelary and surrogate functions to make capital productive and earning power grow in the underproductive who have only their labor power with which to participate in production and earn income. It must prohibit the sterilization and morbidization of capital ownership by those who seek too much capital-productive power. Those two responsibilities are the same function viewed from different sides.

Say's Law asserts that the aggregate cost of the payments to each participant in production for his or her productive input equals the personal income received by all participants in production: an identity, or tautology, as Maynard Keynes pointed out. The total amount of income distributed to all participants is automatically adjusted by the free-market mechanism to equal the market value of the goods and services produced during the period.

Figure 4-1 also makes clear that a free-market economy operates on a type of double-entry bookkeeping. The aggregate market value of goods and services produced becomes the gross national product on the left side of the ledger, and the payments made to the participants in production for their productive inputs become the aggregate consumer income on the right side. An amount equal to the value of all goods and services produced is distributed as personal incomes to the producers. The purchasing power distributed by the market process, *if used for consumption,* is adequate to purchase the full output at current market prices. Any consumers who do not participate in production during the period do not participate in the economic distribution of income.

Economists have been at loggerheads over Say's Law ever since its promulgation in 1803. One of its implications is that the phenomena variously known as depressions, panics, and recessions cannot occur. But they have occurred, and with ever deepening severity, from the inception of the Industrial Revolution. Say's Law has remained a riddle to conventional economists because they approach it with a wrong assumption: that there is only one way that individuals can make productive input and earn income — through labor.

Only when it is recognized that individual persons play the game of supply and demand and that the acquisition and ownership of capital goods by individuals is a subject for governmental intervention and regulation does Say's Law reveal its meaning for an industrial society: Individuals participating in production and earning income through their privately owned capital (ownership of stock in corporations or otherwise), are legitimately engaged in production. They are *capital* workers. (See Figure 4–2.)

Let us suppose that the individual producer in Figure 4–2 is a member of the Forbes Four Hundred, with capital assets of $150 million or more. That portion of capital-earned income not used to buy consumer goods and residences will be invested to earn more income. Given the attenuation of stockholders' property rights (see Chapter 12, pages 123–31), let us say that this $150 million investment yields annual after tax earnings of $10 million. Will the producer and his or her household consume that amount in goods and services, annually, year after year? It is hardly possible. The family may live luxuriously indeed on a modest part of these earnings, spending $1 million or possibly as much as $5 million. But the rest will most certainly be invested in the most productive capital assets (and tax shelters) that skilled advisers can find. This will further increase the owner's excess capital income rather than channel

Figure 4-2. Say's Law Corrected to Recognize Both Labor Work and Capital Work.

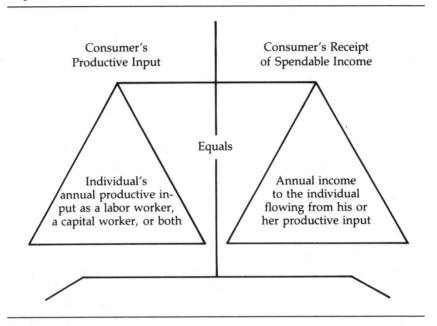

it back into the system as payment for consumer goods and services. Such excess income has thus been sterilized with regard to the production-consumption market. It can only be used to acquire more producer goods. When capital instruments are viewed as a means to produce goods and services vicariously, wealth concentration appears in an entirely new light.

Recognizing that the effect of industrialization is to make production ever more capital intensive and less labor intensive, let us recapitulate the propositions illustrated by the foregoing two diagrams:

- Personal income can be earned in a market economy only by engaging in production, and it is proportioned by the market process to the market value of the respective productive inputs.
- A participant in production who, through his or her superproductive power (normally excess capital accumulation),

earns more income than he chooses to devote to consumption, *necessarily* beggars his neighbors.

• Only what is produced can be consumed.

• One who produces can earn, but only in proportion to his productive input.

• Sustained economic prosperity in a market economy requires that earners and their dependents devote currently earned income to current consumption.

• Thus the income that a market economy automatically distributes to the participants in production to support their consumption will be diminished by the sterilization of capital productive power owned by those who will not and cannot legitimately use it for consumption.

Morbid Capital

The double-entry bookkeeping logic of a market economy for any given period equates the market value of goods and services produced by each participant in production with the income distributed to him or her out of the process of production. It follows, therefore, that income *in excess* of that used for consumption, whatever the reason for the excess, can and will be used only to acquire additional capital productive power, which will in turn produce further excess income, which in turn will be used to acquire still more excess capital productive power, and so on ad infinitum. Such excess productive power can be termed *morbid capital* because its nature, like that of cancerous cells, is to grow without symbiotic relationship to the organism to which it is attached.

Morbid capital is a graphic name for a phenomenon that is explicitly articulated in the British common law of property, which became part of the American common law of property with the adoption of the U.S. Constitution in 1789. It relates to two limitations on the rights that a person possesses with respect to a thing he or she owns. Specifically, a private property owner may not (1) use that property to cause injury to the property or person of another, or (2) use that property in ways that injure the public interest or the public welfare.

Morbid capital does not benefit its owner, who cannot or will not consume what it earns. Moreover, it beggars others by depriving them of the economic opportunity to increase their earnings as capital workers. Morbid capital is contrary to the public interest because it compels coercive redistribution of higher incomes, through taxation and other legislative and labor union measures, to support those who have been made underproductive and nonproductive. The result is social strife, personal suffering and degradation, the erosion of freedom, and ultimately anarchy, which brings on totalitarian government.

There are other motives for accumulating excess productive power besides those having to do with present or future consumption. One of the most compelling is fear of economic collapse, always a danger in unstable, one-factor market economies. Or the motive may be greed or the love of power.

In a mature capitalist democracy, labor-earned income ordinarily would not be needed or used for capital asset acquisition. Commercially insured capital credit would be used instead. The costs of a capital asset would be defrayed in the financing process before its income yield would become available for personal use. Thus the economy would no longer have to choose between current consumption and capital investment—an artificial necessity that has long depressed market demand in Western industrial societies.[1]

Over-earning in order to engage in charitable redistribution to individuals is in conflict with the democratic ideal and goal of personal autonomy; of the rights to life, liberty, and the pursuit of economic happiness not just for some but for all members of the community. Welfare, private charity, boondoggle employment, and other modes of redistribution might well be necessary as temporary political or emergency expedients. But once the democratic capitalist goals have been attained, charity and other forms of redistribution should no longer be needed.

The support of the arts, universities, libraries, parks, recreational facilities, and other public amenities would be one of the highest priorities of democratic capitalism. But this would be accomplished in ways that would greatly reduce the necessity for philanthropic support. Artists, musicians, actors, dancers, and other such professionals would receive much of their income from their private capital ownership. Facilities such as theatres and concert halls would be privately owned, perhaps in part by performing artists. Thus, art and culture should be liberated from parasitic dependence on either rich patrons or state bureaucrats.

Finally, a democratic capitalist economy cannot tolerate the accumulation of excess capital productive power motivated by sheer love of power over others or invidious greed. Not only is this contrary to the principle of limitation, but it violates the logic of free-market economics and the common law limitations of property ownership.

NOTE

1. Since it is a fundamental axiom of conventional economics that an economy must make an absolute choice between consumption and capital formation, many readers, the authors have learned from years of debate and discussion, may have difficulty understanding the implications of this paragraph. A full explanation will be presented in Chapters 5 and 11.

CHAPTER 5

An Analysis of
Conventional Finance

If you are a poor man now, Amaeliano, a poor man you
will always be. Riches nowadays are bestowed only on
the rich.

—*Martial*, First Century A.D.

In his landmark book *Capital in the American Economy: Its Formation
and Financing* Simon Kuznets explains the purpose of finance:

Business units often have opportunities requiring capital investment
much greater than the savings they can withhold from current profits.
Governments may be under pressure for additions to capital equipment
on a scale that far exceeds their ability to collect revenues by taxation or
other means. Consequently, a fairly elaborate institutional machinery
is needed to channel the savings generated among some units in the
economy into the opportunities for capital formation elsewhere. For the
would-be capital users, this is the problem of financing; for the savers,
it is the problem of investing advantageously; and for the comunity, it is
the problem of utilizing savings to enhance the prospects of economic
growth and minimize the dangers of economic instability.[1]

This explanation illuminates the conceptual blind spot at the
core of conventional business finance. Kuznets' point is that businesses have a need for capital instruments before they have saved
the money to buy them. It is the capital instruments themselves
that, once acquired, will earn the costs of their own formation or
purchase. But the consumer's dilemma is precisely the same. In
order to improve his or her economic well-being, the ordinary consumer needs to acquire capital. The consumer, too, lacks the necessary savings—ironically, it is the capital itself that will earn those.
Although bankers responded to the need of business and created
modern business finance, they remained oblivious of the parallel

need of the consumer for capital credit. In response to the consumer's chronic need for more buying power, quite a different institution was invented: consumer credit. But this expedient not only fails to raise the consumer's earning power, it actually reduces his purchasing power by the amount of interest paid.

Economic activity does not begin with human needs and wants for material necessities and comforts. It begins when human needs and wants are matched by the purchasing power to satisfy them; in other words, it begins with consumer demand. But in a market economy, consumer demand begins with consumers' participation in production. That is how consumer purchasing power is earned. In assuming that employment-generated purchasing power will be adequate, both from the consumer's standpoint and the economy's, conventional finance makes a disastrous error and compounds it by ignoring the massive contradictory evidence. If consumers could afford to buy the economy's output from their employment earnings, income redistribution through government-levied taxes would be unnecessary. People would not need welfare, open or concealed. Consumer credit would not be desired, or even tolerated. No one derives consumer satisfaction by paying interest to others.

The conventional investment banking industry and business in general neglect the question of how and where the consumer gets the money to buy. Instead they continue to pin their hopes of profits and prosperity on the very labor income that their activities and policies are capping at its source. Meanwhile, the only other way consumers can earn income to supplement their always inadequate buying power is by acquiring capital ownership and becoming capital workers. But conventional finance makes capital credit available only to the well capitalized and prevents the undercapitalized from legitimately acquiring capital.

Insuring Business Risk

Preindustrial mercantilists invented insurance to cope with the problems of business risk. By charging premiums to entrepreneurs and enterprises subject to specific hazards, they created a reserve fund to defray the costs of those casualties that did occur. Some casualty insurance businesses are conducted for profit, usually through stock companies. Others are in essence cooperative or mutual schemes, designed to protect or indemnify only their own members or insureds. Capital credit insurance is well known in the insurance industry, but because savings-based financing dominates capital acquisitions, commercial capital credit insurance is limited to a few highly specialized areas such as those insured by:

- The Federal Deposit Insurance Corporation, a federal government corporation insuring bank deposits up to $100,000
- The Federal Savings and Loan Insurance Corporation, a federal government insurance agency covering savings and loan deposits up to $100,000 each
- Private mortgage insurance written by a dozen or so corporations in the United States, covering mortgages and mortgage-backed securities
- Municipal debt securities insurance, written by private corporations
- Quasi-government credit insurance involved in transactions like the federal government's bailout of New York City, Chrysler Corporation, Lockheed Corporation, the Federal Farm Credit Banks, and their affiliates
- The Federal Reserve Bank in bailing out Continental Illinois Bank and other banks where substantial amounts of deposits exceed the limit insured by Federal Deposit Insurance Corporation
- Financial Security Assurance, Inc., a recently organized private corporation to insure investment grade credits backed by marketable assets, having a projected insurance capacity of $2 billion of credits per year

But there is another type of casualty insurance that differs radically from commercial casualty insurance. It may more accurately be called illusory casualty insurance because it depends not on spreading the risks insured over a wide area but on concentrating the risks covered in well-financed and relatively powerful enterprises. It is *self insurance*. It relies on the internal financial strength of the self-insurer rather than on the size of the population insured. Therefore, its use is confined to enterprises financially able to absorb the particular casualty losses that they have chosen to self-insure, usually after concluding that the long-term cost will be cheaper than the cost of commercial casualty insurance over the same period.

Self-insurance of feasibility risks involved in capital acquisition transactions has dominated the history of capital financing for reasons arising from our institutional pretense that only labor workers participate in production for the purpose of earning income; that capital is merely a catalytic agent that "raises the productivity of labor," even though labor workers own none of it; and that so long as there is plenty of capital around, it makes no functional difference who owns it. Self-insurance of the feasibility risk leads to endlessly concentrating capital ownership or capital worker power in a fixed (or shrinking) elite class. The result is an economy in which free-market principles no longer apply or work because producing power and earning power are no longer democratically distributed as they were in the natural scheme of things before industrialization.

Democratic financing of capital acquisitions will correct the specific abuses of conventional finance that fail to raise the legitimate earning power of capitalless people to levels consonant with the state of industrialization: internal cash-flow financing, debt financing repaid out of internal cash flow, and sales of equity and debt financing to the tiny minority who already own virtually all nonresidential savings. We will examine the financing methods of democratic capitalism in Chapters 6 through 10 and the replacement of the self-insurance of conventional capital financing with commercially insured capital credit insurance in Chapter 11.

Traditionally, entrepreneurial risk has been insured by the pledging or mortgaging of assets, not just the new assets being acquired but by an equal or greater value of other assets called *collateral*. The entrepreneur may invest his or her own funds in the stock of the business, loan money to the business, guarantee repayment of its debts to others who loan the necessary funds, or, for a consideration, induce others to do one or more of these things. Such methods give the lender a double assurance. Not only will the productive power of the business itself be committed to the repayment of any debt incurred, but additional collateral is pledged to repay the funds advanced to acquire the new assets.

In *The New Capitalists*,[2] Kelso and Adler demonstrated that collateralization to repay capital debt, or investment by the asset buyer of accumulated savings as a down payment, is a way of self-insuring the business risk or capital credit risk. But, they pointed out, this virtually exclusive method of insuring the business credit risk in capital acquisitions has the side effect of denying non-capital owners—the overwhelming majority of the population—access to capital credit and therefore to capital ownership. To insure entrepreneurial risk exclusively through existing assets or previously accumulated savings assures that newly formed or newly acquired capital automatically becomes owned by the owners of those savings and assets—the few who have historically owned all nonresidential capital in the economy. Asset-based finance, as conventionally practiced, is therefore one of the great obstacles to changing the way consumers participate in production to correspond with the technological changes in the production process itself.

The three- to five-year cycle for capital cost recovery is characteristic in market economies as they are presently structured. There is no way to foretell how much greater the rate of new capital formation—the growth rate of the economy as a whole—would be or could be if new capital formation were financed through methods based on democratic capitalist principles. We may be certain, however, that capital cost recovery periods would be substantially shortened and economic growth would be accelerated.[3]

Financing in General

The logic of capital formation and acquisition can be compressed into a single word: self-financeability. If capital instruments did not repay their formation costs many times over, every step in the Industrial Revolution, as well as in the toolmaking age that preceded it, would have lowered the standard of living of the people involved. In the preindustrial world, with its narrow margins of subsistence, that would simply have meant extinction.

Before the decision is made to invest in land, structures, machines, or capital intangibles for any business enterprise, three questions are always asked:

1. Will these assets produce net earnings sufficient to repay their up-front costs (equity investment) within a reasonable period of time (three to five years is a rule of thumb in good times) and then earn enough to finance proper maintenance, depreciation, and periodic renewal (all of which are deductible from gross earnings before net profits are determined)?
2. Will the anticipated net profit return favorably compare with that of other business opportunities?

3. Will the anticipated net income amortize any remaining debt financing and then continue to produce a satisfactory rate of net income for the owners?

It is the responsibility of corporate management or the independent entrepreneur to make these judgments. The basis will be experience, reliable advice, and a financial analysis of all relevant data. The probability that this estimate of the future will prove correct is variously called the *entrepreneurial risk*, the *feasibility risk*, the *business risk*, and the *capital credit risk*. The art of management is to minimize that risk as much as is humanly possible.

Financing, as it relates to capital assets, is the name given to the contractual arrangements made to harness, for the benefit of acquirers, this characteristic ability of capital assets, in well-managed enterprises, to throw off sufficient income to pay their acquisition costs and then to continue, for indefinite periods of time, to return to their owners satisfactory net profits. So essential is this characteristic to businessmen and entrepreneurs of all kinds that, in effect, it imposes a sort of birth control on new capital formation and mitigates against ill-considered acquisitions of capital instruments. If, in the judgment of the prospective capital acquirer or of those who might finance the acquisition, the projected yield of the assets in question will not defray their purchase costs within a reasonable time, the entrepreneurs will not make the acquisition or the prospective lenders will not grant the necessary funding. The penalty for judgment errors on these matters is notoriously high, and properly so. One of management's most basic functions is to determine accurately in advance the feasibility of new investments.

The length of the original cost recovery cycle, and of each subsequent period required for capital to yield a net amount equal to the original acquisition cost, varies, of course, with the economic environment in which production and consumption take place. If an income tax diverts part of the yield of the capital instruments before it reaches the capital owners, the capital-cost recovery cycles will be longer. If national economic policy specifically encourages the *production* of capital goods, as the economic policies of the United States and other market economies (supply-side economics) have done in the past, and leaves the earning of consumer incomes to the progressively diminishing value of labor and ever burgeoning welfare, then the price-recovery cycle will be greatly lengthened. Consumer demand is the fuel of the business engine and a catalyst of capital formation, asset acquisitions, and economic growth in general. Sound economic growth in a free-market democracy can be attained only when the production of goods and services increases in response to the needs and wants of the people, and when their earning power rises spontaneously as production expands, with a minimum of reliance upon friction-generating income redistribution.

The problem with conventional financing techniques is that they address only the productive power of enterprise and the enhancement of the earning power of the rich minority. Sustaining or increasing the earning power of the majority of consumers who are dependent entirely upon the earnings of their labor, or upon welfare, is left to government or governmentally assisted redistribution of income and to chance.

The Economy's Invisible Structure

As the authors pointed out in an earlier book, an economy does not consist merely of the physical things that confront the eye in an industrial landscape—the factories, office buildings, machines and equipment, electrical power grids, planted fields and grazing cattle, oil and gas storage tanks, railroads, ships, loading docks, and the myriad other capital instruments that produce some good or service to add to the economy's gross national product. Behind the economy's visible structure of land, concrete, glass, and steel stands an invisible structure made up of contractual relationships. This is the domain of the entrepreneur, investment banker, corporation lawyer, commercial banker, accountant, corporate manager, labor leader, and the owners of raw materials or other physical capital—the architects of the economy's institutional design. These are the people who weave the detailed web of rights, powers, and privileges along with the reciprocal duties, liabilities, and limitations that connect labor workers and capital workers with the production of goods and services in the visible economy and, in the process, determine the income share each will receive as measured by his or her personal productive contribution. The invisible structure precedes the visible structure in time because those who participate in the production of wealth refuse to commit themselves to an enterprise until they learn what they must contribute to it and what they will receive from it in return.[4]

Most of the shortcomings of an industrial market economy can be traced to defects in its invisible structures. If the structure does not connect particular families or individuals with specific productive processes in the visible economy, then it de facto excludes these people from legitimate economic participation. They are not entitled to receive an income share automatically from the process of production as labor or capital workers. They will have to derive their consumption from something other than legitimate productive input—welfare, perhaps, or through some illegal activity.

If it is possible, through the accepted workings of an economy, to acquire wealth without (1) producing it, (2) owning something that increases in market value or, (3) being the beneficiary of a voluntary gift, the organization of the invisible structure is *per se* defective. It is not designed to keep just accounts between the individuals engaging in production and consumption, but to facilitate fraud and theft.... The invisible sector produces no wealth, but if it contains defects, it may and often does enable those who produce no wealth to acquire it.[5]

The design of the invisible structure must reflect the equational relationship between a population composed of labor workers and capital workers as producers of goods and services and those identical individuals and their dependents as consumers of goods and services. Those responsible for the democratic integrity of a market economy must continually ask: Can the labor workers and capital workers of every household, operating within competitive markets, earn the income required to provide it with the goods and services that comprise a reasonable, self-chosen lifestyle? If not, what can be done? In most cases, the answer will be: Improve the access of the economically underpowered to capital credit.

It is not enough to solve the problem of production, to achieve, to whatever degree, a level of output that policymakers deem satisfactory in the aggregate. The problem of how each family obtains its spending money must also be solved. Historically, the Western industrial economies have left that problem to chance. We have failed to close the circle by not recognizing that as the production of goods and services constantly changes from labor intensive to capital intensive, the sources of consumer income must make the same transition.

When Kuznets published his work in 1961, the ownership of all nonresidential capital in the U.S. economy was in the top 5 percent of wealthholders—just as it was in 1789 and just as it is today.

Kuznets might have seen that savings-based financing is an economically suicidal method of insuring *any* capital credit risks. It deprives business of customers, customers of affluence, and the economy of consumer demand.

Had he considered the consumer's need to become a capital worker, Kuznets might have discovered one of the most momentous secrets of democratic capitalism: *simulfinancing*. This is the idea that each expenditure of funds that acquires assets for a corporation can and should simultaneously acquire a like value of capital ownership for financially underpowered consumers. If both of these objectives are simultaneously accomplished with the *same* investment, then an unimagined new efficiency is achieved for economic activity in a free-market economy.

Thus, the logic of a market economy itself, that legitimate income must be earned by participation in production, requires a form of capital credit that both finances capital transactions for business *and* provides credit for the acquisition of capital ownership by individuals who will use its income to support their consumption of goods and services.

NOTES

1. Simon Kuznets, *Capital in the American Economy: Its Formation and Financing* (Princeton: Princeton University Press, 1961), p. 20. See also pp. 19–29 and 394–99.
2. Louis O. Kelso and Mortimer J. Adler, *The New Capitalists* (New York: Random House, 1961).
3. See the discussion of the true productiveness of capital, pp. 124–30.
4. Louis O. Kelso and Patricia Hetter, *Two-Factor Theory: The Economics of Reality* (New York: Random House, 1967), Chapter 10.
5. Ibid., p. 51.

PART II

GETTING THERE

CHAPTER 6

Financing Tools for Democratizing Capitalism

Blake's Law:
He who would do good to another
must do it in Minute Particulars.
General Good is the plea of the
scoundrel, hypocrite and flatterer,
For Art and Science cannot exist
but in minutely organized Particulars.
— *William Blake,* ca. 1818–1820

Capital acquisition by capitalless American families in today's economy should begin with the federal government acknowledging its obligation to make capital ownership economically purchasable and formally adopting a two-factor national economic policy.

Government's medium for economically democratizing a sparsely capitalized population in an already heavily industrialized economy is capital credit. Capital credit is the one agent powerful enough to accomplish the task within the framework of a private-property, free-market democracy. Moreover, capital credit has been the primary engine of industrialization so far, as well as the chief cause of the institutional deformities that have created and maintained two incompatible classes: the overcapitalized and the undercapitalized.

Each of the financing methods presented in this and the following chapters is based upon the logic of a now familiar financing vehicle, the Employee Stock Ownership Plan, or ESOP. When properly designed and used, the ESOP is a capital credit device for using a corporation's credit simultaneously to finance its own growth and asset acquisition, while enabling its employees, who are its natural stockholders, to buy its stock and to pay for it out of the wages of their newly acquired capital rather than out of the wages of their labor, as has been the case historically.

The task of making capital workers out of the undercapitalized population as a whole, however, cannot end with the employees of private sector corporations. That would exclude the many millions of people who have the same rights and aspirations as corporate employees: people who work for the various functions of government and nonprofit enterprises and associations; those who carry on the activities of the professions and the arts; those who work at scholarly and intellectual pursuits; and finally, the elderly and infirm. Today the latter have little choice but to burden consumers and taxpayers with their support, but they could and should be supported by their own capital.

Nor can the task be limited only to capital assets of the privately owned economy. All capital assets — whether land, structures, machines, or capital intangibles, whatever their present form of ownership — are by nature capable of being privately owned in discrete shares, with their use or services paid for by their primary users and beneficiaries. All capital assets deserve the maintenance, care, interest, and renewal that private ownership fosters. The revenues that would flow from their privatization should contribute to the life-supporting capital structure of the economy.

A Historical Note on ESOPs

Although Louis Kelso had long been certain that financing techniques could be devised to enable people to buy capital and pay for it out of *its* own income stream, instead of from *their* own inadequate paychecks and savings, it was not until 1956 that he found an opportunity to test his hypothesis.

The publisher of a profitable suburban newspaper chain in Palo Alto, California, had promised his employees that when he was ready to retire they would have first chance to buy the business before it was offered to outsiders. When that day came, lawyers and bankers were summoned to work out the means by which the employees could buy out the three major stockholders. In due course, the experts announced their findings. If the employees would commit themselves to maximum payroll deductions, pool their total savings, borrow as much as possible, mortgage or second-mortgage their homes, and cut their living standards to the bone, they could just manage to pay the interest on the loan. They would never be able to repay the principal. There was simply no way for the employees to become newspaper owners. The experts could do no more than advise the employees to forget their "American Dream," get down to work, and hope that their new boss would turn out to be as good a fellow as their former one.

At this point, Kelso volunteered to try his hand. The result was the first Employee Stock Ownership Plan (ESOP). Through it, the newspaper employees were able to buy 72 percent of the stock without touching a penny of their paychecks or savings. (The remaining 28 percent was purchased outside of the ESOP by certain employees, who paid for it out of their personal assets.) Both the ESOP's loan and interest were paid off almost twice as fast as originally scheduled—in eight and one-half years instead of fifteen. Over the life of the trust, the ESOP earned many millions of dollars for employees who, without it, were destined to remain capitalless.

To avoid openly confronting a deeply entrenched national economic policy committed to toil and welfare for the many and capital ownership for the few, this first ESOP was introduced and steered through the various regulatory agencies under the disguise of an employee benefit plan. Thus the principle of enabling employees to buy the employer's business on leveraged capital credit was established first at the federal and then at the state (California) level without arousing either judicial or administrative alarm. The Peninsula Newspapers' ESOP became the Trojan Horse for democratizing American capitalism.

As opportunities arose throughout the next decade and a half, Kelso launched seven more ESOPs, each designed to solve a specific business problem. Although the number of ESOPs began to increase exponentially, it was not until 1974 that the ESOP was given specific recognition in federal and state laws. Senator Russell Long, then chairman of the Senate Finance Committee, engineered this breakthrough. Thus, after a thirty-year struggle, the ESOP is now accepted in the financial world. It won acceptance because—and only because—it solved problems that the entrenched methods could not, or it solved them more efficiently.

Each employee buy-out of all or part of a business enterprise involves a human interest story—and often a cliff-hanger. ESOPs have revived dying companies and even resurrected dead ones. They have served as in-house white knights, enabling corporations to fight off potentially destructive takeover attempts by transferring ownership of major interests in corporations to those who are their natural shareholders: the employees. They have enabled employees of successful companies to achieve lifetime employment, beginning as labor workers, gradually evolving into concurrent labor and capital workers, and then, when they retire from the labor market, continuing as capital workers. Currently, there are an estimated 7,000 ESOPs with an estimated ten million employee participants.[1] Some of these plans have been designed and operated with great respect for the two-factor logic of the theory of democratized capitalism. Others have been properly designed and installed, but thereafter corrupted by management's greed or labor unions' arrogance or failure to dispel an adversarial attitude between management and labor. ESOPs that have been carefully structured and installed by knowledgeable ESOP investment bankers in companies dedicated to the principles and philosophy of democratizing economic power have been resoundingly successful.

Therefore it is not surprising that the ESOP, although it has fought and continues to battle professional and bureaucratic opposition from many quarters, has won friends in Congress, in the media, and among the public at large. When people who fear that they might never again have an opportunity to work reopen a factory or foundry, not as employees but as employee-owners, the entire community rejoices with them and their families. When an ESOP enables managers and rank-and-file employees of a corporation about to be sold to some marauding conglomerate or morbid capital manipulator to emancipate themselves by buying the firm themselves, without having to deplete their bank accounts or paychecks, and thereafter to run it successfully, many lives are transformed for the better. Incidents like these are now becoming commonplace.

Today's ESOPs can only suggest the potential performance of ESOP-financed businesses in a democratized capitalist economy, where capital costs of financing expansion and acquisitions would be low by current standards, and where the barriers erected by a defective national economic policy would have been eliminated. Even successful ESOPs only hint at how much healthier and more prosperous the economy would be had the ESOP been employed years ago. The massive income redistribution of the past half century would have been unnecessary. Technological progress would be decades ahead of its present state. America's chief international economic competitors would still be trying to match the prices and quality of its goods and services rather than overpowering its dominance in a hundred or more of its most important industries. Poverty would have been conquered because the social attack would have been directed against its cause rather than merely against its effects.

When consumer earning power is systematically acquired in the course of the normal operations of the economy by people who need and want more consumer goods and services, the production of goods and services should rise to unprecedented levels; prices of goods and services should tend to be and remain low; the quality and craftsmanship of goods and services, freed of the cornercutting imposed by the chronic shortage of consumer purchasing power, should return to their former high levels; competition should be brisk; and the purchasing power of money should remain stable year after year. Pride of craftsmanship will again distinguish American products.

Much of the discussion that follows in this and the next three chapters is necessarily technical since both financial practice and the tax code are made up of "minutely organized Particulars." Anyone wishing to be professionally involved in the democratization of economic power in the United States must expend the mental effort required to master the subject. But general readers are under no such constraint. Those not concerned with technical implementation or the formulation of laws to make these techniques more attractive and useful can absorb the general message of the book without closely attending to these details. General readers should chiefly be concerned with satisfying themselves that the techniques for democratizing capitalism can in fact accomplish what the authors claim they can: make capital ownership accessible to those who are not and never will be autonomous capital workers by means of conventional finance.

Overview of the Financing Tools

The financing tools we have developed to revamp the U.S. economy fall into several categories based upon the criteria used in selecting their ownership constituencies.

The first category has *functionally* selected stockholder constituencies, that is, target stockholders selected because of their functional relationship to the corporations involved. The ESOP's targeted constituents are corporate employees, present and future. Indeed, in the case of corporations whose pension plans provide occasional benefit increases for former employees, those could also be included, with slight modifications of the law by Congress. A variation of the ESOP is the Mutual Stock Ownership Plan (MUSOP), intended for small groups of corporations—perhaps in related businesses. The third of the function-oriented financing mechanisms is the Consumer Stock Ownership Plan (CSOP). This capitalist version of the socialist consumer cooperative generates stock ownership for its customers in proportion to their patronage. These three function-based financing vehicles are discussed in Chapter 7.

Because of its unusual character, the General Stock Ownership Plan (GSOP) is separately discussed in Chapter 8. The GSOP is intended to include as stockholder-constituents all qualified persons, that is, persons politically selected within specific geographic areas, under constitutional safeguards of equal protection of the laws and equal privileges and immunities.

Chapter 9 describes three categories of financing techniques, each of which legislatively identifies, again under constitutional safeguards, the economically underpowered consumers targeted for stock ownership. These are the Individual Capital Ownership Plan (ICOP), the Commercial Capital Ownership Plan (COMCOP), and the Public Capital Ownership Plan (PUBCOP). An important aspect of these financing methods is that they may be used by Congress to motivate, insure, or reward particular attributes of economic conduct such as merit, craftsmanship, diligence, technical achievement, excellence, or the performance of particularly difficult or unpleasant tasks that have not yet been automated. In other words, ICOPs, COMCOPs, or PUBCOPs can be used not just to fulfill the human rights of economically underproductive people to become self-supporting, but also to implement public policy.

Finally, Chapter 10 describes Residential Capital Ownership Plan (RECOP) financing. Almost every family needs and wants a home—a good home. But homes have mixed characteristics. They clearly are capital instruments because, if soundly designed and well built, they can render dwelling service to their owners for many decades. Yet because their output of dwelling service is normally consumed only by the owning family, and because they yield a particular service and not cash income, they also bear some resemblance to consumer goods.

Each of these eight methods is a capital financing tool. That is, it is a tool for financing new capital formation or for financing the acquisition of existing capital assets or both, while it simultaneously raises the capital-oriented earning power of otherwise economically underpowered consumers. Each tool deliberately generates, through the financing process itself, capital ownership for various classes or types of individuals in the order of priority set by national economic policy. At this writing, only the ESOP has the benefit of reasonably healthy legislative support and significant business use.

For now at least, these eight tools would seem to give businesses, individuals, and governments the full range and flexibility they need to democratize the U.S. economy and to operate it thereafter on private-property, free-market logic. Each method can be adapted to particular situations as they arise. Indeed, several variations of ESOPs are already in use. Entirely new methods employing the same underlying principles and goals may well be invented as experience with the basic concepts grows.

NOTE

1. This estimate comes from Jonathan Feldman and Corey Rosen, *Employee Benefits in Employee Stock Ownership Plans: How Does the Average Worker Fare?* (Arlington, Virg.: National Center for Employee Ownership, September 1985), p. 4. An interim Briefing Report issued in February 1986 by the U.S. General Accounting Office on employee stock ownership plans estimated that 5,188 ESOPs were active, but this report omitted those formed in 1984 and 1985. GAO-PEMD-86-4BR, p. 8.

CHAPTER 7

The ESOP, MUSOP, and CSOP

> Ownership by employees is the only successful system
> for big business. A man has to have more interest than
> his salary to produce the best that is in him.
> —*A.P. Giannini, 1927*

The Employee Stock Ownership Plan (ESOP)

Of the eight financing tools designed to redemocratize the U.S. economy, only the ESOP has gained some visibility in the business world. Its growing acceptance should make it easier to introduce the others.

Figure 7-1 shows how the basic ESOP works.

Let us assume that a corporation, either publicly or privately owned, decides to add to its capital facilities (and its labor force, if necessary) by building or acquiring a plant. A feasibility analysis shows that it can profitably market 20 percent more products or services. The analysis also shows the amount of financing that the expansion will require for the new assets and for increased working capital. Management and stockholders accept the message of democratic capitalism: Conduct your business so that, while protecting your stockholders' property in capital, you raise the earning power of employees and offer all of them who perform well the opportunity for lifetime employment. This is a proper function of the corporation. Employees rightfully expect that as technology makes it increasingly easier to turn out goods and services, they should be able to enjoy better economic lives without having to demand more pay for ever less work.

Management (upon its own initiative or at the request of a labor union) decides to engage experienced ESOP merchant bankers to implement an ESOP financing plan similar to the one diagramed in Figure 7-1.

Figure 7-1. The Employee Stock Ownership Plan (ESOP).

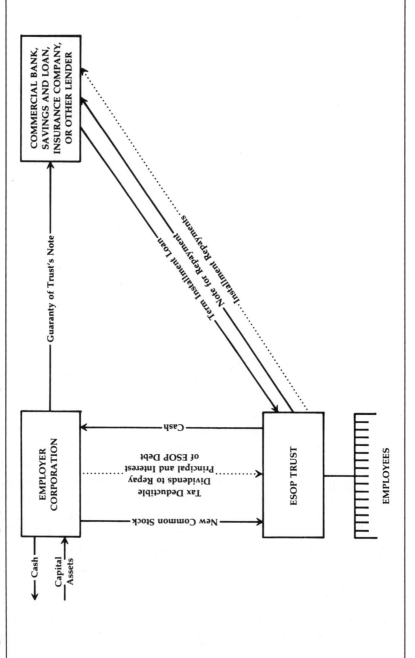

There are several important aspects of the ESOP financing technique, as used for this purpose.

1. The loan is not made directly to the corporation, as under conventional financing, but to an ESOP trust that qualifies as a tax-exempt employee constituency trust under the appropriate federal and state tax laws. Such trusts normally cover all employees of the corporation. Formulas designed into the trusts proportion the relative interests of employees in the stock acquired through ESOP financing to their relative annual compensations from the employer over the period during which each financing is to be paid off. Normally, a committee of three to five persons, appointed by the board of directors, manages the trust. Its membership may include one or more rank-and-file employees.

2. The ESOP committee uses the loan proceeds to buy newly issued stock from the corporation at its current fair market value or, if the stock is not sufficiently traded in a public market to have a market value, at fair value determined by expert appraisal under appropriate Treasury and Labor Department regulations.

3. The trust gives the lender its note for the loan amount. The note may or may not be secured by a pledge of the stock. If so secured, the pledge is designed to release periodically as much of the stock as each installment pays for. The released stock is allocated, or provisionally allocated subject to a vesting schedule, to each participant's account. The corporation guarantees to repay the loan by making adequate payments into the trust for this purpose. The loan may, of course, be secured by any method that the corporation and the lender might have agreed upon had the debt been the corporation's own direct obligation.

4. One aspect of the investment banking art of designing and counseling corporations and ESOP trustees is to structure all loan terms so as to assure that the pre-tax yield of the assets represented by the stock purchased by the ESOP will amortize the principal and interest on the financing, and that any temporary asset dilution of other stockholders will be promptly restored before dividends are paid through the ESOP to the employee shareholders.

5. Banks are beginning to accord greater eligibility to ESOP financing because of the corporation's ability to repay both principal and interest of the loan in pre-tax dollars and to obtain the benefits of simulfinancing. Simulfinancing reduces the earnings cost of capital acquisitions in part because of the ESOP's access to pre-tax

corporate earnings and also because the ESOP saves both the employer's and employees' Social Security taxes on sums used to pay for employees' stock purchased through the ESOP. In addition the ESOP pays for the employees' stock out of the same (simultaneous) investment that buys assets and saves taxes for the corporation and defers income taxes on the employees. The ESOP can also free the corporation from the cost of purchasing low-yield, secondhand securities for pension or profit-sharing plans that do not directly benefit the employer and earn a minimal yield, if any, for employees. Finally, the ESOP gives the employees capital gains treatment on the value of the assets taken out of the trust upon retirement or separation to the extent that the value exceeds the amounts paid by the trust for the stock involved.

6. All income taxation of employees on the value of ESOP-acquired stock is deferred from the time the ESOP pays for their stock until the time the employee retires or separates from the employer. Thus, to the degree that a corporation is owned by its employees through a properly designed ESOP and the ESOP is used to finance its growth, the corporation and its employees can achieve several hundred percent greater efficiency in the use of corporate earnings for capital purposes than through conventional internal financing.

Lenders are partial to ESOP-financed loans for another reason: the higher motivation that results when employees acquire an ownership stake in the employer's business, provided they understand the logic of the ESOP and how it works for their benefit. Congress, in the Employee Stock Ownership Act of 1984, further encouraged ESOP financing by reducing by 50 percent the income tax banks pay on interest earned from loans made to finance ESOPs. When financing is expedited through commercially insured capital credit monetized by Federal Reserve discounting of the trust's note, that additional step would be taken at the closing on the loan.

Assuming that a corporation has a good profit record, which it expects to continue, and that it is in (or within its loss carry-forward period will be in) about a 50 percent combined federal and state corporate income tax bracket, including the employer's share in Social Security taxes, ESOP financing is twice as well secured and twice as easy to amortize as a loan made directly to the corporation, since it is repayable in pre-tax cash flow rather than in after-tax funds. Because of these considerations, conventional collateral and interest requirements should become far more favorable to

ESOP financing than to other types of loans. For corporations in a lower income tax bracket, the tax advantage will, of course, be smaller. Even so, the simulfinancing advantages will be significant. Furthermore, when the corporation finances its own growth simultaneously and automatically, it fortifies the capital-oriented earning power of employees and puts them on the road to lifetime employment. Commercial lenders should be sensitive to these considerations, which are an inherent part of the lending business. Regulatory authorities are in a position to encourage sensitivity where it is lacking.

7. The corporation guarantees the lender that it will make fixed periodic payments into the trust in amounts sufficient to enable the trust to amortize its debt. Within the limits specified by law,[1] such payments are deductible from corporate income taxes. Thus the lender has the general credit of the corporation to support repayment of the loan plus the added security that the loan is repayable in pre-tax dollars. If the design of the financing arrangements and the investment banking skills used to structure the financing conform to principles of democratized capitalism, the corporation's pre-tax return on the per-share equity represented by the stock held in the trust normally will pay off the financing indebtedness within the term of the ESOP's debt. Thus, ordinarily there will be no economic dilution of the equity interest of existing stockholders. If such dilution should occur in a situation where the ESOP financing conforms to ESOP investment banking criteria, it would be only temporary—a year or two—after which the expansion would generally enrich all shareholders.

Under current corporate income tax laws and conventional property-attenuation of corporate shareholders,[2] the corporation's payment into the ESOP trust during the financing period recognizes a far higher degree of private property in the corporate stock beneficially owned by employee stockholders through their ESOP than the directors or income tax–collecting governments observe for non-employee stockholders. Under current corporate tax laws and corporate dividend policies, once ESOP financing is paid off, unless most of the corporation's stock is owned by employees through an ESOP, the ESOP participants will receive only the same fractional wages (dividends) on their investment (that particular block of stock) that other stockholders receive. After all, each share of stock of a particular class is identical and thus is entitled to the same dividends. Until the private property of all stockholders, employee and non-employee alike, is recognized by the full payout of each proportionate share of periodic net earnings, the earnings plowed in from paid-up employee-owned stock, as from non–employee-owned stock, benefit all stockholders.

As an economy begins to conform its financing practices to the concept of democratized capitalism, the full wages of capital will be paid out to all stockholders, and new capital formation will thereafter be financed primarily, and ultimately entirely, through relatively low-cost, commercially-insured capital credit used in conjunction with one or more of the two-factor financing devices.

8. Periodically, stock thus paid for by the corporation is allocated among the participants' accounts in proportion to their relative compensations from the employer corporation for that year. The employees are thus enabled to acquire stock in increments over a period of years at a price fixed when each particular block of stock is purchased by the ESOP trust, with no outlay of their past savings or deductions from their paychecks, and with no brokerage or other charges. The value of the stock thus paid for becomes each employee's currently generated "savings," painlessly purchased out of the income earned by the assets represented by his ESOP stock. This conforms to the general logic of corporate finance, which requires capital to be purchased out of its income yield. But it is innovative in that the ESOP extends this logic to *all* employees.

9. As the financing is completed and the loan paid off, beneficial ownership of the stock passes to the employees. They then have the right to vote the stock, unless the ESOP provides otherwise with the employees' acquiescence, in order to meet temporary conditions imposed by capital lenders or the terms of the ESOP trust. Trusts may be designed to permit the ultimate withdrawal of the portfolio accumulated by employees in kind or in cash, subject to vesting provisions, either at termination of employment or upon disability or retirement. However, it is desirable to design the ESOP and trust so that any dividend income on shares of stock that have been paid for through the financing process and allocated to the employees' accounts will be either applied to the payment for stock being purchased for those employees or distributed currently to the employee-participants as the wages of their capital.

Dividends on the stock held for employees in ESOPs can be paid in pre-tax dollars, thanks to the Employee Stock Ownership Act of 1984. Thus, where the dividends are paid through the ESOP, the wages of capital have the same tax deductibility as the wages of labor.

As the property rights of stockholders to receive the full wages of their capital are recognized, employees will derive a major and growing share of their income from their corporate stock ownership. Upon retirement, their comfort and security will be largely underwritten by income from this source or at least, assuming subsequent diversification, from capital originally acquired in this manner.

10. Once stock of the employer corporation has been bought and paid for through the ESOP, the portfolio can, if the ESOP committee wishes to do so, be diversified by selling company shares and purchasing other suitable investments. This can be done without triggering recognition of income taxes. The arguments for and against diversification will vary in each case. The plan documents can be drawn so as to authorize diversification.

Undoubtedly, Congress or regulatory authorities could improve the powers of ESOP trustees to bring about diversification of the capital portfolio of employees once it has grown large enough to contribute adequately to the employee's lifetime employment. But everyone should keep in mind that lifetime employment is the primary goal.

More frequently, however, where corporations are wholly or primarily employee-owned through an ESOP, the ESOP and the corporation function as an internal stock market for ESOP-financed stock as employees retire or terminate employment. This helps diversify the employees' capital portfolios as they become primarily capital workers. It also enables the ESOP to rotate ownership of the corporation through successive generations of employees and enables management to select its successors as it has traditionally done.

Employees are natural stockholders for the employer corporation's stock. Once an ESOP is established, a large part, if not all, of the corporation's capital growth should be financed through it. The extent to which this is done will vary with individual circumstances. It will also vary with the availability of other two-factor financing methods that may give particular corporations access to other constituencies. The potential advantages of acquiring other stockholding constituencies—customers through CSOPs, tenants through PUBCOPs, residents of particular states or municipalities through GSOPs, or many types of economically underpowered individuals through ICOPs—will be evident as we review the characteristics of each of these financing methods.

Federal and state governments have the power to make particular capital financing methods more attractive. By using this power, they will be discharging their pragmatic and constitutional obligation to ensure that every citizen is economically autonomous and able to earn the income needed to support a reasonable standard of living as long as he or she lives.

The Mutual Stock Ownership Plan (MUSOP)

Some corporations are simply too small to afford the professional and administrative costs of a carefully prepared ESOP; their number of employees or scale of operations is not large enough to justify the expense. This may be true even when ESOP financing in successful and well-managed companies, irrespective of size, can be accomplished through commercially insured capital credit and monetized through Federal Reserve discounting in order to give these companies and their employees access to low-cost credit.

In such cases, and perhaps in many other situations, the legislative authority to establish and use Mutual Stock Ownership Plans may be desirable. Even in the case of medium-sized businesses, the MUSOP may be attractive for simplifying procedures, reducing costs, diversifying investment without losing simulfinancing advantages, and consolidating the internal stock market functions for repurchase of stocks when stockholders wish to sell.

MUSOPs would be designed to function mutually for the corporations needing access to reliable, low-cost capital credit to finance their growth and working capital. They would also serve as a means of efficiently building ownership of diversified portfolios of stocks, including their own stock and stocks of similar corporations, for their employees.

Once commercially insured capital credit becomes available, MUSOPs would borrow from lending sources qualified to discount eligible loans with the Federal Reserve Bank. Such funds would be individually invested in newly issued stock of each MUSOP-financed corporation. Using the same principles employed by the ESOP, equivalent value in the stock of the MUSOP would be allocated to the employees of that corporation as each corporate loan is paid off.

Thus the MUSOP would become a sort of super-constituency trust for the employees of several corporations. It would provide the diversification of a mutual fund for the employees of those corporations, as well as an efficient means of financing the corporations themselves. MUSOPs would presumably earn the income to defray their operational costs from service charges to participating corporations. Full payout of corporate net earnings by each participating corporation would be made regularly to the MUSOP, which in turn would pay over the dividends to its stockholders.

The design and operation of a MUSOP are illustrated in Figure 7-2.

MUSOPs could be local, regional, or even national, according to the needs of corporate participants and their respective employees. The management of each MUSOP trust would normally be selected from the managements of the participating corporations.

The Consumer Stock Ownership Plan (CSOP)

The CSOP is the capitalist equivalent of the socialist-derived producer cooperative. To date, only one CSOP has been created, but its success was spectacular. This was a chemical fertilizer company named Valley Nitrogen Producers, Inc., headquartered in Fresno, California. The establishment and financing of that corporation as a CSOP took place between the years 1957 and 1963. Valley Nitrogen made it possible for farmer-stockholders to acquire ownership of two new chemical fertilizer plants that promptly paid for themselves and thereafter, in effect, enabled the farmer-stockholders to buy their enormous supplies of chemical fertilizers at little more than production cost, since profits were paid out to stockholders in dividends. Oligopolies, incensed by the competition of a farmer-owned business that cut fertilizer prices by more than half, persuaded Congress to change the tax laws so that the first CSOP would be the last one. What Congress has taken away, however, it may, upon reflection, decide to restore.

Figure 7-2. The Mutual Stock Ownership Plan (MUSOP).

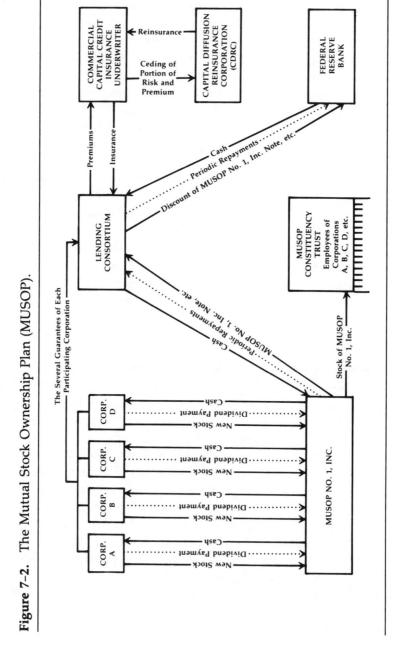

The CSOP technique is intended to build capital ownership into consumers of public utilities and of other business corporations having monopolistic or oligopolistic consumer relationships, or having a substantial body of steady consumers who purchase its goods or services in large quantities year after year.

1. A constituency trust, with an account for each individual customer of the corporation, is established with any designated bank or trust company, or within the corporation itself.

2. By law, the corporation—whether a bank, public utility, insurance company, or other suitable corporation—would be given the power, as a condition of patronage, to require each of its individual (noncorporate)[3] service or product consumers to subscribe to his or her proportionate part (based on his or her relative estimated purchases of the corporation's goods or services) of a ten-year, moving average capital budget of the corporation. This capital budget would cover total estimated capital formation, acquisition, and working capital requirements, except those financed through the corporation's ESOP or other democratic capitalist financing method. Aggregate payments by customers on their subscriptions, offered by the corporation to its customers or potential customers from time to time as financing requirements dictate, would be synchronized with cash flow requirements so as to enable stockholders to meet their subscription payments by applying their dividends, or whatever portion of them may be required, on their stock purchase accounts. Methods can be designed to adjust subscriptions for over- or underestimation of the consumer's product purchases.

3. Funds for the payment of each consumer's subscription would be provided by a consortium of banks, insurance companies, and perhaps savings and loan firms.

4. The number of shares subscribed by each consumer would be determined by each consumer's projected proportionate patronage of the corporation's publicly offered services or products. Each subscription would be payable solely from corporate dividends, representing the full or substantially full payout of the wages of the capital represented by the stock thus purchased.

5. As soon as commercially insured capital credit, monetized through Federal Reserve discounting, becomes available for CSOP financing, a CSOP-financed corporation should be legally required to make a full payout of the proportionate earnings to its stock-

holders and to finance its future expansion and working capital requirements by stock sales to its CSOP and its ESOP. Dividends should be made tax deductible by the corporation at both state and federal levels, as is the case with the ESOP.

6. The corporation's ESOP and CSOP loan paper would be made directly discountable with the Federal Reserve Bank by the corporation's financing lenders at the minimal discount rate based on the Federal Reserve's annual operating costs.

7. Once commercially insured capital credit becomes available to CSOP financing of suitable corporations, we estimate that the effective interest rate to the borrower, the CSOP trust, should not exceed 4 percent, including competitive bank compensation for making and servicing the loan, insurance premiums for loan insurance, and Federal Reserve discount.[4]

8. Until the corporation's stock has been paid for on a share-by-share basis, the dividends received should be made nontaxable to the buyer. This is part of the logic of the ESOP. However, as the stock is paid for, again on a share-by-share basis, the dividends would become taxable income to the consumer. They would have the effect of offsetting (reducing) the consumer's cost of services purchased from the corporation.

9. Thus a combination of ESOP and CSOP financing in public utility and other appropriate corporations would tend to hold down production costs. Employees and consumers would be fortified with rising capital worker incomes. Employees would be motivated to restrain their demands for progressively more pay in return for progressively less work. Consumer earning power generally would be expanded, particularly the power to buy products and services of the CSOP-financed corporations.

The design and operation of a CSOP are shown in Figure 7–3.

Everyone, of course, is a consumer. But for CSOP financing to be practical, the participant should be a long-term, habitual customer. Moreover, the products or services bought from the supplier business should require a significant part of the consumer's income, since the amount of stock that consumer will acquire is related to his or her CSOP purchases.

In the case of regulated public utilities that enjoy monopoly or near-monopoly status, both logic and fairness compel the use of the CSOP financing technique. As things are today, consumers are obliged to pay the cost of all traditional public utility capital

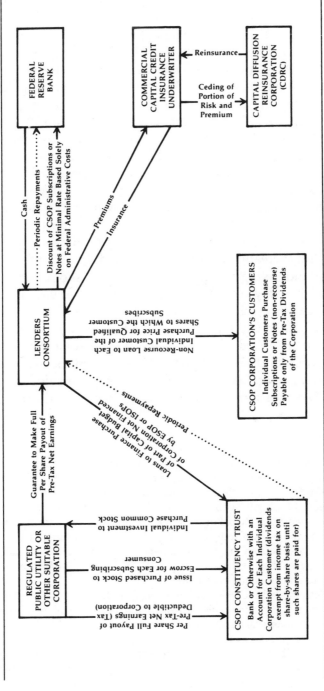

Figure 7-3. The Consumer Stock Ownership Plan (CSOP).

expansion. But consumers acquire no capital ownership in the utility; they merely finance capital ownership for the utility's absentee shareholders. Thus traditional utility financing enriches the already affluent owners who put their capital to work providing services to captive consumers, while it adds nothing to the income-earning power of those consumers. This practice is both illogical and discriminatory. A good case can be made that it violates, among other principles, the 14th Amendment of the U.S. Constitution, which guarantees equal protection of the laws—in this instance, the laws governing access to capital credit.

The success of Valley Nitrogen Producers, Inc., a CSOP producer of agricultural chemicals in California, stemmed from the fact that the stockholdings acquired by each of its statewide body of stockholders were proportioned to their individual fertilizer requirements. Very substantial dividends first paid for each stockholder's stock, and thereafter significantly reduced his or her fertilizer costs.

The underlying principles of the CSOP should have wide application in every economy. In the United States virtually all banks, insurance companies, and public utilities are ideal candidates. So are retail merchandizing chains such as Sears, Roebuck & Co., Montgomery Ward, Saks Fifth Avenue, Dayton–Hudson Corporation, Standard Oil Company, Alcoa, Mobil, Safeway, Great Atlantic and Pacific Tea Company, as well as diversified food producers such as Pillsbury Mills, Standard Brands, and Beatrice Foods.

NOTES

1. The limit of annual tax deductible payment by the corporation into the ESOP is now 25 percent of annual covered payroll. The annual amount of payments into the ESOP for the benefit of individual employees is currently limited to 36 percent of individual compensation. Both of these limits apply only to funds used to reduce principal of the ESOP's loan. All payments used to defray interest may be deducted by the corporation without limit. These limitations are carryovers from the employee-benefit legislation that was adapted to use for ESOPs. They serve no reasonable purpose and should be abolished in favor of management's discretion.
2. See "Capital Is Much More Productive Than It Appears," pp. 124–29.
3. All capitalist financing tools are designed to build capital ownership into individual, economically underpowered consumers in viable holdings that do not violate the principle of limitation. The essence of democratizing capitalism is to make all business and industry operate for the advantage of specific individual capital owners and to make such capital ownership accessible to all families. The objective is to restore, at a higher level of productiveness, the

human scale of economic activity that existed in preindustrial society. This objective would be confused or defeated if corporations, along with individual consumers, were eligible participants in the constituency trusts of CSOPs or other capital theory financing entities.

4. Four percent represents the real interest rate to a borrower for democratic capital financing purposes. This rate will be made possible through commercially insured capital credit (see Chapter 11).

CHAPTER 8

The GSOP

When the machine displaces man and does most of the
work, who will own the machines and receive the rich
dividends?
— *Justice William O. Douglas, 1962*

The General Stock Ownership Plan (GSOP) is a method of providing broad categories of undercapitalized individuals with access to capital credit in the course of providing financing for types
of businesses that fall within the scope of the particular authoriz-
ing legislation. Federal law could authorize a GSOP where its scope
of activities is to be national or regional, and both federal and state
law where its scope is regional, statewide, or limited to one or more
municipalities. Eligibility for financing by a particular GSOP or
type of GSOP would be based on geographical residence and on
other relevant criteria.

The GSOP could be used, for example, to build ownership of
major gas, oil, or coal transmission lines into all economically underpowered citizens in the states through which they might pass or
into Social Security recipients in those states, under transition formulas that would reduce Social Security payments as their GSOP
dividends rise.[1] It could also be used to privatize publicly owned
productive facilities, like the postal service, by putting ownership into specified classes of economically underpowered consumers. Other individuals who might be made eligible for financed
acquisition of a GSOP's stock would be unemployed parents of
dependent children, physically or mentally handicapped individuals, technologically displaced workers, and retired military
service personnel. Each GSOP would be a private corporation organized to acquire, through commercially insured capital credit
financing, own, and operate productive assets for its stockholder
constituents.

The AGSOC Experiment

Both the federal General Stock Ownership Corporation law of 1978 and the proposed (but not adopted) Alaskan matching law were pioneering experiments with the concept of the General Stock Ownership Plan.[2] The Alaskan General Stock Ownership Corporation (AGSOC) was authorized by federal law[3] but never activated because the state of Alaska failed to enact the necessary matching state legislation. Since this is the closest that a GSOP has yet come to implementation, however, we may use the AGSOC proposal to illustrate one application of basic GSOP principles.[4] Figure 8-1 shows the AGSOC plan schematic.[5]

1. Payment would be made by AGSOC of the cash initially required to close the transaction. AGSOC's loan financing (see 9 below) would provide AGSOC with the cash necessary to pay BP Pipeline, Inc. its cash requirement for the assets to be acquired by AGSOC and would enable AGSOC to retain necessary working capital.

2. It was tentatively proposed that one share of AGSOC stock would be issued to the AGSOC Trust and Escrow Division for each eligible individual prior to its acquisition of any operating assets or anything of net asset value, so that the initial issuance in escrow would merely be the acquisition of a right to indefinite future value and thus not constitute an income taxable event to the shareholders. A U.S. Treasury ruling to this effect would have been sought prior to the issue of stock. All shares issued by AGSOC would have been held in escrows established for each individual resident as of the time of such purchase, as "resident" would have been defined by the state legislature. As valuable assets were acquired by AGSOC, the shares beneficially or directly owned by stockholders would acquire value. The terms of the escrow would have been established by AGSOC's bylaws or by rules and regulations adopted pursuant thereto. The escrow of initially issued stock would continue at least until expiration of the nontransferability period of five years established by Title VI of the Internal Revenue Code, until the age of majority under Alaskan law (presently age 19) for underage stockholders, and until shareholders had complied with reasonable AGSOC rules and regulations covering release of the stock from escrow. While full details could have been developed only by the AGSOC board of directors, it is reasonable

Figure 8-1. The AGSOC Purchase of the Interest of BP Pipeline, Inc. in the TransAlaska Pipeline (TAPS).

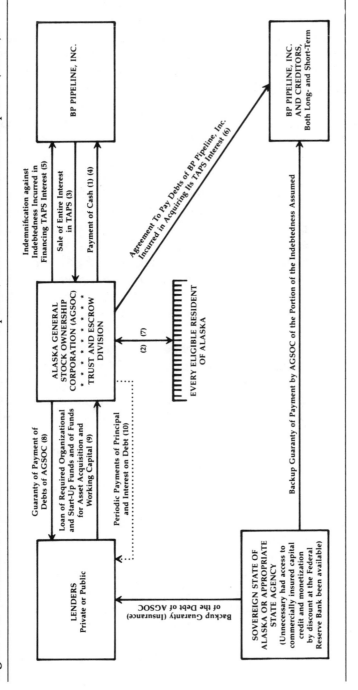

to assume that AGSOC would have facilitated transfers of stock between individuals for stock ultimately released from escrow. It is, of course, a political question as to how qualified residents, for purposes of the plan, would be defined. The character of the federal GSOC law was such that AGSOC could have operated much like a closed-end investment fund.

3. This diagram is based on the assumption that the entire interest of BP Pipeline, Inc. in TAPS would have been purchased by AGSOC. There was also evidence that the seller would have been willing to negotiate a sale of 12.5 percent interest in TAPS rather than 15.8 percent. Many considerations would enter into the board of directors' decision of whether to buy 12.5 percent or a greater amount, including the relationship of the Alaskan oil interest in the resulting AGSOC carrier capacity, the economics of transporting for others, and AGSOC's resulting marketing problems.

4. Preliminary financial data suggested that the seller would sell its interest at a price that would make it whole, assuming that other TAPS owners did not exercise their preferential rights. Presumably this figure would be adjusted, depending on negotiations and the closing date.

5. AGSOC, under this financial design, would agree to hold the seller harmless from liability for any of its outstanding debt of $1.212 billion.

6. AGSOC would have assumed the obligation to pay the outstanding debts incurred in connection with the seller's acquisition of its interest in TAPS.

7. The hatch marks represent, in the aggregate, each of the qualified residents of the state of Alaska whose eligibility would have been defined by the Alaska General Stock Ownership enabling law. Each resident would have had an individual escrow account in the escrow facility built into AGSOC by its enabling legislation and bylaws. It should not be an objection to the plan as a whole that the purchase of a single asset, or even of several substantial assets for a defined body of qualified residents, might not solve all of the economic problems of Alaskan residents.

8. AGSOC would have directly guaranteed the repayment to the lenders of funds loaned to AGSOC initially and from time to time thereafter.

9. The lenders would initially loan AGSOC the cash required for organization, staffing, and start-up of operations, as well as funds

for the acquisition of operating assets and initial working capital. This illustration assumes the making of guarantees within limitations set forth in the Alaska GSOC law and in other applicable law pledging the general credit of the state of Alaska or, alternatively, obtaining adequate credit insurance from the Alaska Permanent Fund, a multibillion-dollar fund receiving state oil royalties, thus obtaining a minimum interest rate. While the guarantee by the state of Alaska of up to 25 percent of the funding, upon proper vote of the citizen shareholders, was contemplated by this proposal, the general credit of AGSOC would, of course, stand behind the entire debt. Were commercially insured capital credit available, and the transaction monetized by discount at the Federal Reserve Bank, no state or state fund guarantee or insurance would have been needed.

10. Federal GSOC law required the payout, as dividends to shareholders, of 90 percent of the pre-tax earnings of AGSOC. Dividends paid by the corporation into AGSOC's Trust and Escrow Division would then have been used to make payments on principal and interest of AGSOC's debts.

At the state level, the AGSOC legislation, in the absence of regulatory authority for commercially insured capital credit financing and monetizing by discounting with the Federal Reserve Bank, contemplated raising funds from banks and other private sources. AGSOC promoters also believed that the state of Alaska or the multibillion-dollar Alaska Permanent Fund would contract the capital diffusion reinsurance necessary to facilitate raising the loan financing for the initial AGSOC investment and working capital.

Before the proposed AGSOC bill was introduced into the Alaska legislature, British Petroleum Company, one of the eight corporations owning the TransAlaska Pipeline Service Corporation (TAPS), let it be known that it was willing to sell to AGSOC its interest in that pipeline, at depreciated book value. In the summer of 1980, key company officials confirmed this offer.

On November 6, 1978, the president signed into law the Revenue Act of 1978, Title VI of which authorized the establishment of General Stock Ownership Corporations (GSOCs) and gave immunity from federal corporate income taxes to corporations specially chartered by state legislatures and conforming to the conditions set forth in the federal law.[6]

Thus, GSOCs organized between January 1, 1979, and January 1, 1984, were granted permanent immunity from federal corporate income tax. The new federal law, however, had one serious shortcoming: The corporate income taxes that would otherwise have been collectible from AGSOC were to be currently borne pro rata by its shareholders, even before AGSOC had finished paying for assets producing the income. Congress assumed that GSOCs could initially invest in income-producing assets of such nature that the combined investment tax credit, capital recovery allowances, and interest costs would eliminate any tax on shareholders during the period of repayment of a GSOP's capital financing costs. Dividends in excess of those deductions against stockholders' personal incomes would be taxed as ordinary income in each particular stockholder's tax bracket. It goes without saying that for consumers who do not own capital, having dividend income that is taxable as personal income, even if used to purchase capital productive power, is better than having no means at all for acquiring income-producing capital. Still, this flawed logic of the first GSOP legislation would have impaired the consumers' purchasing power by the extent of the state and federal income taxes imposed on earnings required to capitalize the stockholders.

Despite the shortcomings of the federal enabling legislation, AGSOC, had it gone into operation, would have provided capital-sourced incomes for all qualifying Alaskans for many decades.

The first federal GSOP law made the initially issued stock of AGSOC nontransferable by the shareholders for five years, except in the case of a shareholder's death or upon his ceasing to be a qualified resident of the incorporating state by, for example, changing his state of residence. The law, emphasizing the importance of the stockholder's future enjoyment of his AGSOC dividends, did not require a shareholder who left the state in which the GSOP was organized to sell, transfer, or forfeit his stock. However, he would not be able to sell or otherwise transfer his share to any person who was not at the time of such transfer a qualified resident of the state of incorporation. The federal law did require that transferees must be individuals, since the purpose of the law was to broaden the ownership of productive capital to every individual resident of the state of incorporation. To accommodate the growing number of Alaska residents ineligible to acquire AGSOC stock because they were not residents on the legislatively set date, new stock issues could have been added from time to time to finance new projects or to improve existing assets, and to take in new residents as stockholders. The whole tenor of both the federal law and the proposed Alaskan enabling law was to inhibit concentration of the ownership of GSOP shares.

Marketability and Sale Value of GSOC Shares

By express provision in the federal law, GSOC shares could be owned only by individuals, and since no individual was permitted to acquire more than ten shares of a GSOC's stock, a public market for the shares, in the traditional casino sense of U.S. public stock markets, would presumably never develop. This would not have meant, however, that limited selling and buying of GSOC shares, which was permitted in the event of a shareholder's death or emigration from the state, could not occur even during the period of the five-year nontransferability restriction imposed by the federal law.

When that need arose, either the seller would find a qualified resident buyer or the shares would be temporarily transferred into a general escrow account in the constituency trust, or to a duly appointed outside transfer and escrow agent, until the seller's representative or a qualified stock broker could find a buyer. In such a case, the broker would be precisely that, bringing seller and buyer together and charging a fee, with the transfer being made directly from the individual seller to the individual buyer.

Our proposed design for AGSOC recommended that during the initial five-year restriction period, sales by emigrants not wishing to retain their AGSOC shares be made at the then current book value. During this five-year period, the corporation would have had the right of first refusal to purchase shares so offered. In addition, the federal law provided that shares in a GSOC could not be pledged, assigned, mortgaged, or subjected to other encumbrances during these five years.

When the five-year period of restricted alienability expired or the shareholder attained majority, whichever occurred later, a strictly *investor* (not speculator) market for GSOC shares would have arisen. During the initial five-year period, the book value price limit on any sale of GSOC stock might have significantly discouraged sales motivated by emigration, and sales of GSOC stock by estates of decedents would have been handled by negotiations between buyers and sellers.

In requiring GSOCs to pay out at least 90 percent of their net income in dividends each year, federal law conferred a high degree of private property upon GSOC shareholders. This imbued the wages of capital from GSOC stock with a measure of the character and sanctity of private property that law has traditionally conferred on the wages of labor. Dividends would have been paid periodically and dependably, if earned. An active and well-conceptualized educational and communications program would have been instituted encouraging shareholders to regard shares not as speculative windfalls, but as capital-worker employment providing them permanent sources of income.

Quarterly valuations of GSOC shares would have been made and speedily communicated to all shareholders. Presumably, therefore, in a free *investor* market, expert appraisal by independent professional appraisers would influence the trading prices of AGSOC stock. In such a market, the investor interest of buyers should dominate. Speculator interest would not be encouraged.

Governance of a GSOC

As private business corporations, GSOCs would have been managed by their boards of directors, which presumably would have hired the most highly qualified professional managers obtainable. Because each GSOC, in the aggregate, would have been owned initially by all residents of the incorporating state, it should have received financial support from the incorporating state or its agencies in several ways. If authorized by the state legislature it could have received loans or guarantees of loans for start-up funds to enable it to organize, hire professional management, pay directors' fees or salaries, negotiate for the acquisition or construction of productive assets, and negotiate financing. Such financing might be made, if properly authorized, by the state, or with guarantees by the state or its agencies. When commercially insured capital credit becomes available for financing that conforms to democratic capitalist principles, GSOCs should be among the first types of corporations to qualify.

In a democratized capitalist economy there should be no limit on the number or amount of capital assets a particular GSOC could acquire, so long as no market monopolies are created and individual capital holdings do not violate the principle of limitation.

NOTES

1. In instances involving Social Security or other welfare income, transition formulas – generous transition formulas – should be instituted so that as capital-earned incomes rise, welfare payments will be reduced. For example, when capital income of a GSOP participant is two or even three times greater than welfare, each dollar of additional capital-earned income might be made to offset a dollar of welfare income. The objective, of course, is the economic autonomy of each family and the elimination of government or governmentally implemented redistribution from taxpayers and consumers.
2. A precursor of the GSOP was first proposed under the name "Financed Capitalist Plan" by Louis O. Kelso and Mortimer J. Adler in *The New Capitalists* (New York: Random House, 1961).
3. Revenue Act of 1978, Title VI, enacting Subchapter U of the Internal Revenue Code.
4. Every aspect of the design proposal, which was prepared by Kelso & Co., Incorporated for the Alaskan Legislative Finance Committee on January 25, 1979, and supplemented by an additional report in February 1980, was subjected to legislative scrutiny, testimony, and criticism by governmental and private witnesses.
5. Paragraph numbers in text correspond to parenthesized numbers in Figure 8-1.
6. Substantial portions of the following discussion of AGSOC have been abstracted from the report of Kelso & Co., Incorporated to the Legislative Finance Committee of the House of Representatives of the State of Alaska, a public document.

CHAPTER 9

The ICOP, COMCOP, and PUBCOP

What is common to the greatest number gets the least amount of care. Men pay most attention to what is their own; they care less for what is common; or at any rate, they care for it only to the extent to which each is individually concerned.

—*Aristotle, 384–322 B.C.*

The Individual Capital Ownership Plan (ICOP)

The ICOP may be the most flexible of all of the two-factor tools. It would give corporations more flexibility in making and keeping consumers economically autonomous in the course of financing business growth. It would enormously facilitate and reduce the costs of financing the growth of small and medium-sized businesses, while enlarging the brokerage and investment banking fraternity's financing opportunities. And it would also provide government's economic policy branches with a sensitive supplementary tool for building economic self-sufficiency into consumers where other financing tools are inadequate or inappropriate.

There are millions of families and individuals who are not employees of prosperous corporations and thus cannot be adequately encapitalized through an ESOP, or who do not work for governments or government agencies and therefore cannot have their earning power adequately raised by the privatization of capital assets now owned by governments. There are millions of consumers who may acquire stock in public utilities whose services they buy, who could become stockholders in those enterprises through CSOP financing to a degree sufficient perhaps to pay their utility bills, but not sufficient—even when combined with other two-factor capital acquisition opportunities that may be opened up to them—to remove them from the rolls of the economically underpowered. Millions of other low-earning families and individuals exist wholly or partly outside the productive order because they are retired and, lacking adequate capital earning power, are forced into deprivation and dependency. In multitudes of other cases consumers may need access to ICOP-financed stock to diversify capital assets in the course of building viable capital earning power.

On the other hand, hundreds of thousands of small and medium-sized businesses will require low-cost, efficient capital financing for which other ownership-democratizing tools are not appropriate. The ICOP, under which eligibility for stock purchase must be determined by the (probably federal) government under constitutional safeguards such as equal protection of the laws, will be one of the most powerful tools for putting the logic of free-market economics to work in democratizing the economy and in maintaining its growth and prosperity.

ICOP financing would enable small and medium-size businesses to market their securities nationally or regionally, as they may wish. Individuals who conform to categories made eligible by legislation and regulations to receive loans for investment in a diversified portfolio of securities of corporations that desire to market their stock to ICOP-financed individuals would apply for such loans through their bank. Bank trustees and representatives of the investment bank selling consortium would, in securities prospectuses, describe securities currently qualified for ICOP financing. They would also counsel applicants for ICOP loan financing on such considerations as diversification, relative yields, risks, and prospects. Presumably, selling prospectuses could be far simpler than those currently required by the Securities and Exchange Commission. These securities, after all, will already have been double-checked. Regulatory agencies will have judged them eligible to obtain commercially insured capital credit loans for individual portfolio buyers and will have qualified them for Federal Reserve discounting of the financing loans.

Figure 9–1 represents one of the simplest ICOP arrangements.

The ICOP would provide societal credit for capital acquisition by individuals meeting governmentally prescribed criteria. The first and most indispensable qualification would be nonownership

Figure 9-1. The Individual Capital Ownership Plan (ICOP).

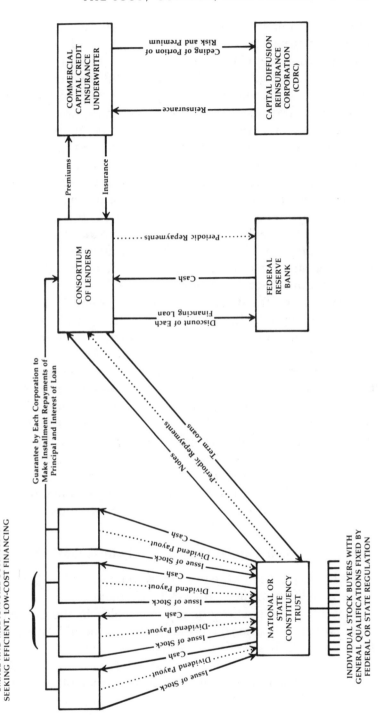

of a viable capital estate. Other considerations might include personal merit (a sort of American Nobel-type award), individual need, residence in a depressed region, or merely that other financing methods described in this book are insufficient or unavailable to the borrower. "Adequate earning power" would have to be legislatively defined as target minimum earning rates for families of various sizes and compositions. As we have noted before, it will be an enormous task to transform an economy where 95 percent of the population is capitalless into a democratized capitalist economy in which every consumer is economically autonomous. Even at economic growth rates of 20 percent or more a year—rates that a democratic capitalist economy should easily attain, so long as poverty remains within its borders—all consumers cannot be transformed from poor to economically self-sufficient overnight, just as everyone cannot pass through even a wide door at the same time.[1] Congress must establish priorities.

In structure, the ICOP would closely resemble the ESOP. One alternative might be the use of common constituency trusts rather than individual ones. In either case, each eligible individual's financed investment could consist of a mixed portfolio of securities in companies seeking and qualifying to finance their expansion through public offerings to ICOP constituency trusts. A key function of the investment or merchant banker in democratic financing would be to assist particular corporations in meeting the requirements to make their loans eligible for commercially insured capital credit insurance and for Federal Reserve discount, to synchronize such financing with the use of ESOP or other two-factor financing methods, and to put together selling groups to market the client corporations' stocks to ICOP borrowers in various markets.

The Commercial Capital Ownership Plan (COMCOP)

What has been said of the objectives to be served by ICOP financing is equally applicable to COMCOP financing.

The largest repository of capital wealth in the United States and in other industrialized economies is commercial buildings and structures. Such structures are the type of wealth most favored by the hoarders of capital. Clearly, the kit of democratization tools would be deficient if it did not include one that allowed financially underpowered consumers – many of whom dwell in owner-occupied, single-family residences – to acquire interests in income-producing commercial structures. This kind of two-factor financing can also be used to diversify capital portfolios of consumers, where this is desirable.

So long as government, business, and professional politicians are oblivious to two-factor economics and to the social necessity for democratized economic power, the incredibly concentrated ownership of commercial real estate will continue to cast a sinister shadow over the economy. Collateralization of previously owned capital will remain the dominant method of financing commercial real estate and structure acquisition, virtually assuring that the more valuable capital holdings are, the more rapidly they will expand and the less relationship there will be between the income the owner can and will spend for consumption purposes and the earning power of his capital holdings.

Nowhere is the power of morbid capital more active and effective than in the real estate lobbies. These lobbies have brought into existence and maintained legislation that radically diminishes – indeed often totally eliminates – taxation on income flowing from real estate, buildings, and structures. Most of these laws have been enacted in good faith by legislators who believed they were increasing labor worker jobs and promoting full employment in obedience to national economic policy. But policy, legislators, and laws have been blind to the constitutional rights of adult American citizens to be economically autonomous and to remain so into their retirement years. So also are our legislators blind to the great number of capital-worker jobs that would arise if capital holdings were required to be financed through two-factor techniques.

It is important to keep in mind that no matter which form acquisition financing takes, the number of labor-worker jobs at any stage of industrial development required to build any particular structure will be the same. The difference that two-factor financing makes is in the number of capital-worker jobs – permanent capital-worker jobs – that it would generate, and which continue indefinitely after construction is complete, and in the vastly greater number of labor worker jobs that a truly flourishing construction industry would require, considering that this industry is the nation's potentially largest employer of labor.

No area of the economy more urgently needs democratic reform than commercial real estate and structure financing. Nowhere in the economy is capital morbidity more rampant or the one-factor perversion of economic activity more potent. Accelerated depreciation allowances, investment credits, tax-free exchanges, deferred taxation, and reduced capital gain taxes are heralded by lobbyists, legislators, and the press alike as ways of promoting employment and economic growth and counteracting depression. All of these groups overlook the fact that most of the "economic growth" such laws encourage is actually growth in morbid capital ownership and concomitant growth in the sterilization of capital income earning power in morbid capital owners.

Commercial Capital Ownership Plan financing is a powerful antidote for capital morbidity in commercial real estate and structures. Vigorously applied, it would do much to democratize the massive concentration characteristic of this sector of the economy. Although COMCOP has many features in common with its conceptual siblings, GSOP, RECOP, and PUBCOP financing, its stockholder constituents need not necessarily be selected on the basis of state or local residency, employment, or purchase of utility or other business product or service. The eligibility criteria should initially be determined by the federal and/or state governments, with entrepreneurs making their own selections within these guidelines, at least until ownership of viable capital estates has become universal. Once that objective is achieved, each COMCOP-financed enterprise might be left free to select its own constituents, as long as the principles of democratic capitalism are observed.

For maximum ease of administration, the constituency trust best suited to COMCOPs would be a corporation that not only passes all income through to its stockholders in dividends but also allocates to them pro rata depreciation, tax credits, and other capital cost recovery allowances.

The general design of a COMCOP financing plan is shown in Figure 9–2.

Unless the COMCOP construction financing is such that it automatically converts into permanent financing when the construction is completed, the permanent financing should conform to the democratized pattern of the interim financing.

COMCOP financing can and should be used to democratize the ownership of the hundreds of thousands of existing structures

Figure 9-2. The Commercial Capital Ownership Plan (COMCOP).

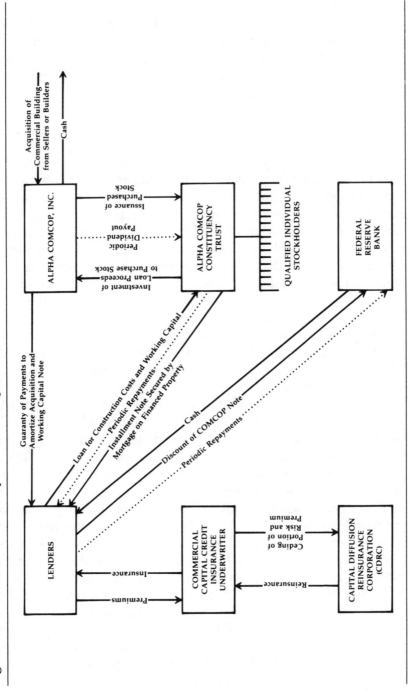

that today are pumping income into morbid capital holdings where it frustrates the interdependency of consumption and production in a free-market economy. Sales out of morbid ownership into democratized ownership could be encouraged by laws that heavily tax morbid income and perhaps by other types of morbidity laws that conform to constitutional safeguards of private property.

The Public Capital Ownership Plan (PUBCOP)

Inherent in the concept of democratic capitalism is the idea that human freedom requires the maximum separation of political and economic power within particular institutions. As we emphasized earlier, economic power is represented by private ownership of labor power by individuals and by the private and individual ownership of capital by those same individuals. Since labor is a diminishing factor of production, at least in comparison with the combined output of capital and labor, and capital an expanding one, economic democracy can be achieved only by increasing the number of individuals who participate in production and earn income through their ownership of capital.

The privatization of the public sector offers innumerable opportunities to realize this goal and in so doing create an economic democracy to bulwark our political democracy.

Publicly used and operated capital facilities include streets, sidewalks, canals, prisons, legislative, administrative and judicial buildings, schools, airports, office buildings, transit systems, port facilities, and the like—anything that under past or present financing methods requires governmental incurrence of debt and governmental acquisition of capital ownership.

The legal vehicle for PUBCOP financing should be private corporations that pay out substantially all of their net income to their shareholders, after initial capital cost recovery allowances and allowances thereafter adequate to maintain and update the assets. While an appropriate governmental body—normally Congress— must decide who will be eligible to purchase stock in PUBCOPs, common sense suggests that individuals residing in the geographical area where each PUBCOP's principal assets are located, and employees of the public body or bodies using or administering the facilities, would hold high priorities for becoming future owners. Further, if the employees of the governmental entities whose capital requirements are being financed by PUBCOPs were included as financed stockholders, for the purpose of providing them lifetime employment, enormous sums in public employee pension costs would be saved.

Our suggested design structure for PUBCOP financing is shown in Figure 9–3.

If, in lieu of capital credit insurance from the public corporation involved, commercial capital credit insurance is obtainable — from insurance companies, in the form of bank letters of credit, or otherwise — then it should be feasible to monetize (without risk) the transaction through Federal Reserve discounting. In that case, public improvements would not be limited directly by the cost or by the availability or capriciousness of loan financing from private or public lenders. Interest and the relevant taxpayer costs of rentals for use of the facilities by the governmental units for which they are intended would be low. The vastly greater flexibility of democratized capitalist financing techniques should also assure that capital ownership by governments, or their agencies in any form, will diminish and finally disappear.

This method should be extremely useful in assisting governments with large holdings of public capital to privatize these assets, liquidate their debts, enhearten their poor, and, in due course, make vast reductions in taxes levied to support welfare and transfer payments, to say nothing of creating democratic economic autonomy.

Taxpayers can maintain local public control over expenditures by voting on whether to lease particular capital instruments, as well as on the suitability, design, rental rate, and so on for the capital improvements in question. Since PUBCOP financing is in essence COMCOP financing (suitable for democratized financing of private commercial structures like apartment houses, office buildings, factory and store facilities, and the like), where the lessee is one or more public entities, the selection between privately owned structures and structures that are either COMCOP or PUBCOP financed would hinge on overall conformity to two-factor implementation methods, the proximity of stockholders to the structures or land, and other public policy considerations.

PUBCOP or COMCOP financing for publicly used capital instruments can be combined with ESOP financing for public employees — presumably those whose employers are involved in the

Figure 9-3. The Public Capital Ownership Plan (PUBCOP).

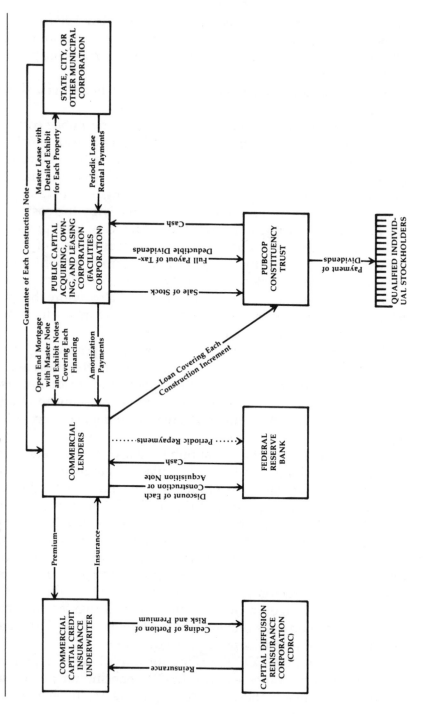

administration or use of such capital. The PUBCOP or COMCOP facilities-owning corporations would hire the employees and "lease" them (probably at cost) to the public entity that leases and operates the facilities. The growing capital ownership acquired by such employees would then constitute an income-producing capital estate designed to supersede the costly and inadequate public pensions that today are a major cause of high taxes, and to be a major step on the way to lifetime employment for them. PUBCOP financing could be designed for the federal government's capital projects, and it, too, could take the place of federal and federal agency public pensions.

PUBCOP financing requires assurance — and this would be one of the guarantees of PUBCOP bond counsel in their opinion on each financing — of a tax base and tax laws adequate to assure payment of rentals by the occupying or using public entities. Amortization payments, principal, and interest on PUBCOP debt, like amortization payments on ESOP financing, should be made deductible from all forms of corporate income taxation.

A Note on Redevelopment and Special Improvements

Redevelopment under state and federal laws enacted to carry out the national full employment policy has been disastrous. It has ruined neighborhoods and lowered the standard of living of the people displaced. In millions of cases, it has made the poor homeless. It has made the rich richer and kept the poor capitalless.

Structurally sound but rundown buildings have been leveled and replaced with shoddy, frail, functionless structures whose only justification is that temporary jobs were created during their construction (and perhaps later in razing them). Some of the displaced poor have been put into subsidized housing, but since they have been afforded no income-earning power, they live in social humiliation and frustration, much of which is expressed in crime.

New York's Harlem and Bedford-Stuyvesant areas are merely two of the most aggravated symptoms of the urban development disease that has caused the destruction and abandonment of thousands of square miles of residential and commercial buildings that could have been fully restored by owners with decent incomes, and that would cost trillions of dollars and decades of time to replace. These desolated areas often enjoy ideal geographical locations.

They could have been preserved and made permanently valuable and charming had viable capital-worker employment been obtained by those who worked and lived in the neighborhoods. Two-factor capital financing tools can, in many of these cases, bring about their restoration and the building of capital-produced incomes into those who become their owners.

The "special improvement districts" that once flourished, often in connection with carefully drafted and skillfully planned zoning laws and building codes, have similarly failed. In the beginning they were amazingly effective in enabling affluent residents of particular neighborhoods and regions to beautify their surroundings. But as the gap between rich and poor grew more ominous after 1930, these laws and institutions of necessity came to be used to tax the rich in order to ameliorate to a small degree the environments of the poor. Thus ended their usefulness and their acceptability to the taxpayers so burdened.

Regional and neighborhood planning and special improvements accomplished by imposing costs on those "benefited" are fundamentally sound. Supported by democratic capital financing tools, they can do for poor neighborhoods now what special improvement districts once did for affluent ones, while raising the poor to affluence without burdening prosperous taxpayers; in other words, without redistribution. Democratic capital financing techniques are enormously important to environmentalists, planning commissions, municipal officials, and others interested in reversing the forces that are making our communities unlivable. Unfortunately, a discussion of their implications is beyond the scope of this book.

Variations and Combinations of Financing Techniques

Most ESOPs have been used independently, that is, not in combination with other methods of democratic capitalist financing. It is unlikely, however, that a CSOP, intended primarily for financing public utilities and creating consumer ownership, will be used independently of an ESOP. Employees would resent a public utility or other corporation that built ownership into its customers but not into them.

A PUBCOP or CSOP, synchronized with an ESOP, could be

used to transfer from the public to the private sector enterprises that properly belong in the latter. Examples are the United States Postal Service, the Tennessee Valley Authority, the atomic energy fuel production enterprises, and government-owned wealth producing enterprises in general. Indeed, each of the financing methods employing capital theory can be combined with any of the others to promote democratic capitalist goals.

Governmental Regulation

It would be premature to address the question of regulatory qualification of equity securities of corporations to be used in capitalist financing methods that receive federal and state legislative authorization. There is no reason, however, to anticipate that whatever problems arise will be insoluble. The major regulatory powers of government in a democratized capitalist economy would be directed toward:

1. Establishing and maintaining the integrity of property
2. Enacting and enforcing laws implementing the principle of participation
3. Enacting and enforcing laws implementing the principle of limitation, primarily by ensuring that, to the maximum extent reasonably possible, capital-sourced earning power grows where it is needed and does not grow where it becomes morbid.

Securities represent much of our society's capital-based earning power, badly allocated though it is. They include not only the savings of the rich, but the petite "savings" of the undercapitalized majority held in pension funds, profit sharing trusts, and other financial intermediaries, all of which tend to keep the poor poor. Why have we allowed the economy's earning power to be used as stakes in a monstrous, zero-sum gambling casino game, operated by the securities industry in the name of "investment?" There is no rational answer to this question. A democratized, free-market economy will simply eliminate this destructive game.

Above all, a democratic economic policy would minimize regulatory barriers that unnecessarily impede the economic transformations necessary to a fully democratized capitalist society.

NOTE

1. The historical growth rate of the economy of 4 to 5 percent has been achieved through one-factor financing methods that directly raise the capital-sourced earning power only of the already capitalized minority and that depend on redistribution to raise the earning power of the uncapitalized majority. It does not seem unreasonable to expect that capital financing methods employing the principle of simulfinancing could accelerate the growth rate to 20 percent.

CHAPTER 10

The RECOP

But as our populations expand, as the worldwide movement from countryside to city embraces all peoples, as
problems of housing and juvenile delinquency rise about
us, have we not the right to ask: is what we are witness-
ing, in essence, not the first consequence of the de-terri-
torialization of man? And if man *is* a territorial animal,
then as we seek to repair his dignity and responsibility
as a human being, should we not first search for means
of restoring his dignity and responsibility as a proprietor?
—*Robert Ardrey*, 1966

The most important form of productive capital most consumers
traditionally acquire, or seek to acquire, is a home. A residence is
a capital structure—a "dwelling machine," to use Le Corbusier's
phrase. It produces marketable wealth. If the consumer did not
own it, he would have to rent its equivalent at a rental value determined by market forces.[1]

Moreover, a well-built house, distinguished by high-quality materials, craftsmanship, architecture, and style, can produce wealth
(living space and use pleasure), not just during the lifetime of one
consumer, but for generations.

Conventional housing finance suffers from the same defects as
every other form of savings-based finance. It is unnecessarily costly
for the rich and economically ruinous, if not utterly useless, to the
poor. It permanently throttles the home-building industry by ty-
ing it to the inadequate financial resources of end-users, who must
resort to loans from banks, savings and loan companies, insurance
companies, savings banks, private lenders, real estate finance companies, mortgage banks, and the like—a finance system that routinely levies interest charges on home loans equal to three to five
times, or more, the purchase price of the house itself.

Residential Capital Ownership Plan (RECOP) financing would recognize that a home is a capital instrument, indeed, to consumers in an economic democracy, a vital capital instrument. It would extend the logic of the ESOP to every family. It would make commercially insured capital credit available to all home buyers.

It is no secret that the American dream of home ownership has now become the impossible dream for most families and single individuals who do not already own a home. And the few houses built in response to the limited effective demand created by mortgage credit are declining in quality. Inflation, chiefly caused by the progressive demands for more and more pay for the same or less work, and interest rates designed primarily to protect lenders and morbid capital owners from inflation, force builders to reduce size, craftsmanship, and amenities in order to cut costs. But this phenomenon is occurring at a time when the nation's technical (as distinguished from financial) home-building capability has never been greater. We have no shortages of the physical things required to build houses—no shortage of resources, labor, know-how, or talent— and certainly no shortage of physical need for housing or for bigger and better housing. Indeed, we have a surplus of building capabilities and building needs. We could expand the economy's present physical capability to build houses and apartments again and again if only those who want and need them had the money to buy them.

RECOP financing would give the home buyer access to low-cost loans, saving the buyer interest costs and financing fees over the loan term that now amount to three to five and more times the purchase price of the home itself. RECOP financing would give the home buyer a deduction from personal income taxes for depreciation and, like other techniques of democratic capital financing, would exempt the income used to acquire a home, (that is, income equal to the home purchase price), from personal income taxation, so long as the buyer does not violate the principle of limitation. Figure 10–1 illustrates RECOP financing.

Conventional Home Finance Compared with RECOP Financing

To illustrate the cost saving in the purchase of a residence using RECOP financing and to compare it with costs under present-day conventional home financing, let us use the example of a $150,000 residence.

Figure 10–1. The Residential Capital Ownership Plan (RECOP).

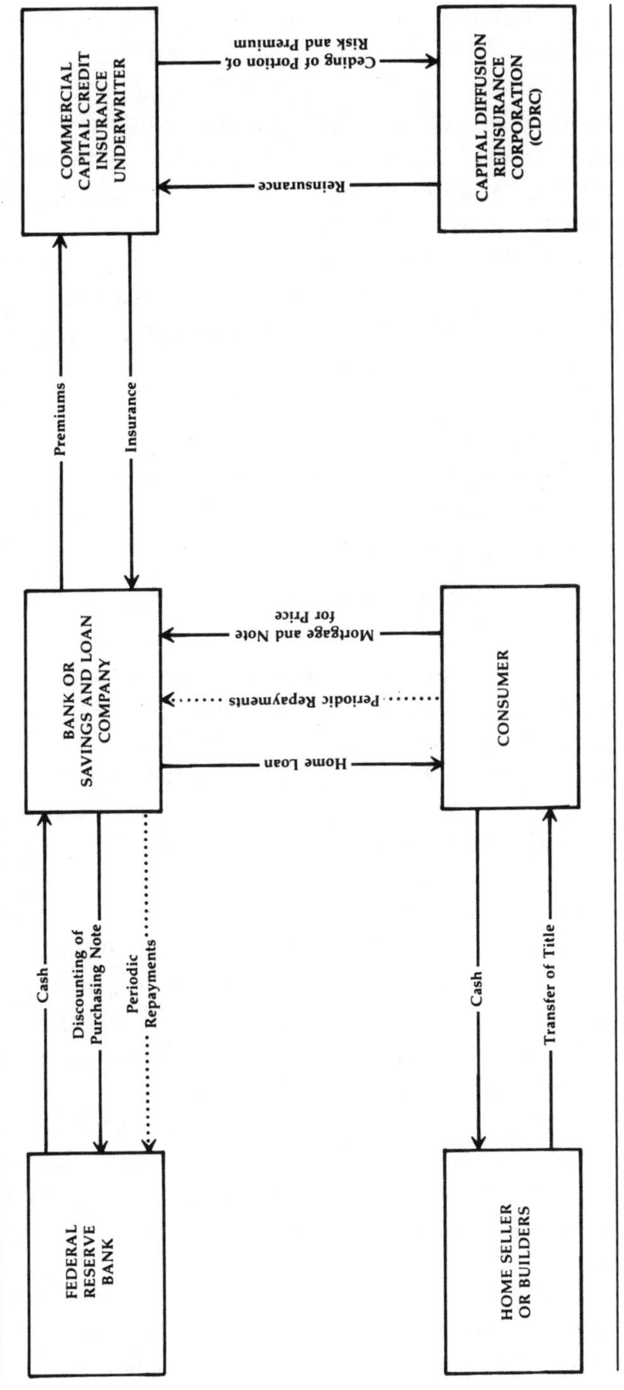

Assume that the purchase in each case is made *entirely* with borrowed funds and that the conventional loan has a 14 percent simple annual interest rate,[2] no down payment, and a thirty-year term amortizable in equal monthly installments covering both principal and interest. The buyers are a couple whose effective personal income tax bracket is 50 percent, including federal, state, and personal Social Security taxes.

Further assume that the RECOP-financed purchase is on the same terms, except for a bank service and insurance fee of 4 percent per annum, made possible through commercially insured and CDRC reinsured capital housing credit.

$150,000 Residence Conventionally Financed

Amount of loan (full amount of purchase price)	$150,000
Total interest paid over 30 years at 14% simple	489,831
Residence cost to purchasers	639,831

$150,000 Residence RECOP Financed

Amount of loan (full amount of purchase price)	$150,000
Total bank service and insurance fees paid over 30 years	100,226
Total saving in interest ($489,831 – $100,226)	389,605
Exemption from taxation of income used for purchase (half the principal only of the original purchase price)	75,000
Total saving of RECOP financing over conventional financing (sum of two preceding lines)	$464,605

RECOP financing of this $150,000 residence would produce a saving of $464,605 — *more than treble the original cost* of the residence.

More important than the *comparative* saving under RECOP financing, however, is the computation of the *actual* net cost to the buyers. This would be the sum of the principal and interest laid out ($150,000 + $100,226 = $250,226) minus the income tax saving (50 percent of purchase price, or $75,000), for a total of $175,226.

Thus the net effective cost to the purchasers of the $150,000 residence, after they receive a deduction from personal income taxes, is a mere *$25,226 more than the original purchase price* of the residence!

In these computations, the saving to residential purchasers using RECOP financing instead of conventional financing and the net effective after-personal-income-tax cost to the purchasers are conservatively stated. Under RECOP financing, the term of the mortgage would probably be ten years or less, resulting in a further saving of more than half of the interest cost. Thus the buyer's out-of-pocket cost of the paid-for residence under RECOP financing could actually be a few dollars *less than the actual purchase price of the house.*

Furthermore, using property tax principles appropriate to a democratic capitalist economy, no real property taxes should be levied upon the residence, or at least upon the portion of the value represented by the unpaid purchase price, during the purchase term. It is counterproductive, from the standpoints of both the individual and government, for the latter to engage in practices that slow the rate at which citizens become economically self-sufficient.

The radical advantage of RECOP financing over conventional financing is no greater than for capital buyers under an ESOP or under any technique of democratic capitalist finance where commercially insured capital credit is available. But the advantages are easier to understand because home buying is a relatively simple and familiar transaction.

Home ownership is a goal for all non-homeowners. Clearly, RECOP financing would make reaching this goal a reality as quickly as the required number of residences could be constructed.

NOTES

1. In past writings and lectures, although with misgivings, we have abided by federal and state tax law interpretations that classify personal residences as consumer goods rather than capital goods. But our acquiescence in the conventional wisdom of course proved wrong. Obviously, family residences are capital goods whose marketable wealth is consumed exclusively by the owners. In a democratized market economy, where a residence would be treated as a capital asset for initial purchase financing, for depreciation, and for all other purposes, and personal income equal to the amount used to purchase it would be free from income taxation, as it is in ESOP financing, a personal residence would pay for itself with dazzling swiftness. The innovation of RECOP financing would require reorienting consumers who do not own their own homes to the economic, psychological, and political importance of home ownership.

2. At this writing mortgage rates are in the 11 percent area. Within the past five years they have been above 20 percent. Unless we correct our flawed, one-factor national economic policy of attempting to make labor work alone suffice to enable consumers to consume goods and services that are partly produced by labor and largely produced by capital, the economy will be forced to increase its reliance upon inflation and other methods of redistribution to function at all.

CHAPTER 11

The Missing Logic of Finance: Commercially Insured Capital Credit

The legitimate object of government, is to do for a community of people, whatever they need to have done, but can not do, *at all*, or can not, *so well do*, for themselves — in their separate, and individual capacities.
— *Abraham Lincoln, 1854*

We have learned that successful capital acquisition, whether of existing or new capital assets, aims at amortizing the acquisition costs out of the net earnings of the newly acquired capital. Further, the risk that the net earnings of the newly acquired capital may not be sufficient to pay off principal and interest of the acquisition costs within the agreed repayment time is, like other business risks, customarily covered by insurance — feasibility risk insurance. And finally, the dominant type of financing feasibility insurance is self-insurance, that is, insurance where the borrower or entrepreneur is required to assume the risk. For example, a company or an entrepreneur acquiring an asset costing $1 million will be able to finance $650,000 of the cost. The acquiring party must provide $350,000 equity financing to cover the feasibility risk and to meet the remaining cost. This practice limits access to capital credit to the small minority of the population that is already capitalized.

Once the national economic policy has been purged of its one-factor error and business has been guided into conformity with the new, two-factor policy, most capital acquisition financing would take place through commercially insured capital credit.[1] Commercially insured capital credit would enable the U.S. economy to regain its lost economic democracy almost imperceptibly and in conformity with the constitutional safeguards to private property, equal protection of the laws, and the rights of life, liberty, and pursuit of economic happiness for all Americans. Economic plutocracy will quietly give way to economic democracy. The United States would be the first industrial society to accomplish this transformation.

Figure 11–1 illustrates what is involved. Note that it requires creation of no new institutions[2]—only intelligent changes in the ways that familiar ones are used.

The numbered paragraphs below correspond to the numbers in Figure 11–1.

1. The corporations that own the capital assets and employ labor workers and capital workers would function, so far as their business, management, and other institutional relations are concerned, just as if they were conventionally financed, except for the changes implicit in the new financing approach. They would have access to pre-tax dollars for capital purposes, they could take advantage of simulfinancing, and they would raise the capital-worker income-earning power of their employees or non-employee stockholder constituents (for CSOP, ICOP, COMCOP and PUBCOP financing) as they expand their own productive power.

2. The constituency trust, like that for employees in the widely used ESOP, would be a common law trust in which all stock-purchasing constituents are beneficiaries. It would be a tax exempt entity that made capital credit available to each employee or other financed stock purchaser to buy the corporation's stock without personal liability and without deductions from savings or paychecks. The constituency trust, in the case of the ESOP, would automatically allocate shares of stock, as they are paid for, to each employee in proportion to his or her relative compensation from the employer. In the case of the constituency trusts in other than ESOP financings, the dividends (fully paid out per-share net income) would be allocated to the principal and interest of the purchase price as they are paid.

3. The commercial bank or other financing lender would be the immediate, but not the ultimate, funding source. Most importantly, it would administer repayment of the credit once the loan has been made. Under commercially insured capital credit financing, this loan-committing and administering function would continue as it has been developed under savings-based capital financing,

Figure 11-1. Democratic Commercially Insured Contract Financing of Capital Transactions.

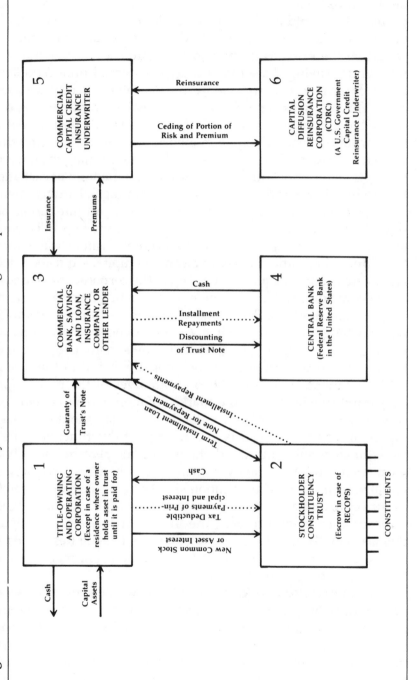

but the bank's source of monetization would change. The bank's profitability would be the same as under traditional financing. In other words, its service fee, which would be competitively limited, would be the same as its true spread (interest rate less inflation rate) under savings-based financing. This would unquestionably assure financing costs well below interest rates of recent decades.

4. Through making ESOP and other two-factor financing discountable by the lender at the Federal Reserve Bank, the central bank would be used solely to monetize the transaction.[3] In other words, the Federal Reserve Bank would be performing the government's constitutional function of providing a medium of exchange for use by all parties to accomplish their contractual arrangement: arranging financing to enable the corporation to acquire certain assets, structuring contractual arrangements so as to take full advantage of simulfinancing, and using the corporation and its labor force to produce goods and services to pay off its capital acquisition debt and interest and to acquire ownership of the corporate stock issued to the constituency trust for the employees or other constituents in individual holdings. The monetization of the contracts involved not only tangibly quantifies them (in accordance with the commitments of the contracting parties), but allows many people to participate in the performance of the obligations and in the receipt of the compensations involved on both sides of the production-consumption equation of the market economy. The Federal Reserve Bank would have no risk; its discount rate should be based purely on its operating costs in carrying out this function, which we estimate would not exceed one-half of one percent annually at most.[4] Since the federal government's economic responsibility to its citizens under the Constitution simply fulfills its responsibility as surrogate for nature in a primitive economy (i.e., to enable them to be productive and to earn the income they need to support themselves), these surrogate services of the Federal Reserve Bank should in no sense be considered a potential profit-making function for the federal government.

5. In due course most casualty insurers would probably seek to underwrite commercial capital credit insurance. By its very nature, credit feasibility insurance, conceptually mishandled in the past largely through self-insurance, would doubtless become the major function of commercial insurance underwriters. To be sure, their ability to lay off a portion, even a major portion, of the risk to a new governmental entity, the Capital Diffusion Reinsurance Cor-

poration (see paragraph 6 below), would undoubtedly be critical until they have gained experience with major commercial insuring of capital credit financing.

The fact is, however, that a very large part of the risk underwritten would be nominal rather than real. The insurance loans made by lenders to ESOP trusts of corporations with substantial net worth are riskless to the extent that the corporation's net worth covers that risk. Corporations, through two-factor techniques, simply expand the risk-insuring use of their assets to benefit mutually themselves and the new stock purchasers, who, incidentally, are consumers in the same market economy in which the corporation expects to sell its products.

Loans made to corporations to finance corporate capital transactions that simultaneously and proportionately raise the income-earning power of employees or other new stock purchasers as consumers, are generally safer and more secure than loans made to finance corporate growth that merely raises the earning power of already well-capitalized stockholders, many of whom will not spend their increased earnings in consumer markets. They also make a far greater contribution to the economy's prosperity. In short, such capital financing conforms both to free market logic and to economic democracy.

6. The federal government would establish the Capital Diffusion Reinsurance Corporation (CDRC) to reinsure any portion of any two-factor financing risk assessed as reasonable and insurable but not already insured by the commercial capital credit insurance underwriters. In establishing CDRC, the federal government would not be undertaking a new responsibility but merely simplifying and rationalizing an existing one.

Federal Responsibility for Economic Prosperity

Is the federal government responsible for the health and prosperity of the American economy? Until the 1930s this was a controversial question, with differences of opinion reverberating throughout the era of New Deal innovation. Today, both voters and officeholders take it for granted that the answer is yes.

The great bulk of all congressional legislation and legislative hearings relate directly or indirectly to economic questions and issues. The president of the United States is elected primarily on his economic views and promises, as are senators and congressmen, governors and state legislators. Each national administration is judged a success or failure on the basis of the degree of economic prosperity for which it can claim credit. State and even city administrations are measured by the same, if less comprehensive, standard. Although virtually indistinguishable once in office, both political parties claim in their campaign rhetoric that the ultimate goal of their differing philosophies is the economic well-being of the ordinary American family.

Any event that threatens the economic interests of the United States, whether it involves relations between the U.S. economy and others or adversely affects a domestic industry, a branch of foreign trade, or a significant block of American citizens, commands immediate government attention. When a major corporation, like Lockheed or Chrysler, or a major municipality, like New York City, is threatened with collapse; when major banks, like Continental Illinois Corporation and its subsidiaries, or the Federal Farm Credit System run into trouble, or major industries, like steel, automobiles, agricultural implements, and hundreds of others, begin to reap the consequences of redistributing income through taxation and the price system, the government concentrates on shoring up another crumbling piece of the U.S. economy.

At issue, then, is not *whether* government will assume responsibility for economic prosperity, but *how* it will choose to discharge its obligation to do so. Congress, having adopted an unsuccessful strategy in the 1930s and having reaffirmed and elaborated upon its error during every subsequent administration, is now deeply enmired in administering a tacit industrial policy rather than taking the initiative in formulating and adopting a realistic economic policy and then overseeing the implementation of that policy. The federal government has abdicated its policy-making and overview functions. It has become, as retiring Senate Majority Leader Howard Baker charged, an "elected bureaucracy."[5]

If every leveraged buyout and every merger and acquisition of one corporation by another were ESOP financed, thereby putting hundreds of thousands of employees every calendar quarter on the road to becoming capital workers, we would have taken a long first step toward democratizing our economy. But business leaders, labor leaders, legislators, and politicians still act as though they do not believe it makes any difference *who* owns the economy's productive capital. Until they wake up to the fact that capital ownership does matter, the concentration of capital ownership in the invisible structure will continue to destroy the economy at a faster and faster rate.

Today we are in a far better position than President Roosevelt was when, in the first shock of the Great Depression, he told the American people, "the only thing we have to fear is fear itself." With the New Deal, and his brilliant leadership, we did strike out boldly to correct an economic policy that had failed. Unfortunately, however, the economic policy we put in its place has also failed, and all signs point to an even more devastating economic collapse than that of the 1930s.

Given this background, there can hardly be any basis for questioning the establishment of the Capital Diffusion Reinsurance Corporation (CDRC) as a U.S. government–backed capital credit reinsurance underwriter, supported by the full faith and credit of the U.S. government. This entity would fulfill a function that is already the government's but that the government is not carrying out in the most rational and purposeful way.

Today, as for the past half century, government has sought to discharge its responsibility for the health and prosperity of the economy through coerced trickle-down; in other words, through redistribution achieved by the rigging of labor prices, by taxation to support redistribution and job "creation," or subsidization by inflation and by all kinds of welfare, open and concealed. Under democratized capitalism, government would substantially assume financial responsibility for the economy through establishing and supervising the implementation of an economic, labor, and business policy of democratized economic power. A fulcrum for this task would be the CDRC. Each financing accomplished through two-factor methods would be subjected to expert hierarchical scrutiny, first by corporate management, then by commercial lending institutions, then by the commercial capital credit insurance underwriters, and, finally, perhaps even by the CDRC and/or the Federal Reserve Bank. The examiners would satisfy themselves that each financing would be able simultaneously to liquidate both its own asset formation or acquisition costs and the costs of making capital workers out of the economically underpowered. The entire design is calculated to negate inflation because it eliminates the chief cause of inflation, namely redistribution.

The democratized market economy proposed herein is designed to avoid the difficulties government now encounters in functioning as the insurer and guarantor of national economic health and prosperity under a lopsided policy that addresses the capital credit problems of business but not the need to restore the democratic earning power of most consumers. That need is as obvious as their need to consume goods and services. Government has too long been called upon to use its overall taxing powers and its powers to encourage "savings" based upon earnings withheld from the markets for goods and services to rescue institutions that can operate efficiently only with broad majority participation in production and the enhanced consumer power resulting.

Thus one of the practical differences between CDRC financing and conventional financing—so far as the function of government is concerned—is that under CDRC financing the government acts positively from the beginning to assure that the loan will be self-liquidating and that it will not depend upon governmentally coerced redistribution to enable consumers to buy what is produced.

The Privileged Class Argument against Democratic Access to Capital Credit

Capital financing lenders historically have rationalized their refusal to grant capital credit to would-be borrowers who are not already well capitalized on the grounds of either unproven reliability or proven unreliability. Commercially insured capital credit substantially eliminates these grounds for disqualification where it is used in connection with any two-factor financing method except Residential Capital Ownership Plan (RECOP) financing. This is true because, as the ESOP illustrates, the investment banking design for ESOP financing commits the institutions involved to channel the earnings from the assets representing the newly purchased stock to the ESOP trust and from the ESOP trust to the lender as loan repayments. These contractual arrangements may be designed either to preclude or to permit the distribution to the stockholders of dividends on shares of stock that have been paid for, although some portion of the debt arising out of the particular financing transaction remains unliquidated. But payment of the purchase price for the shares, together with any interest or service fees thereon, is made without personal intervention of the financed stock purchaser. The design of the invisible structure of the employer corporation in each type of two-factor financing (except for the RECOP) assures the loan repayment out of its operations, so long as the business is successful, and by the capital credit insurers to the extent of any default.

The 1984 amendments to the then existing ESOP legislation, which specifically make dividends on ESOP-held stock income tax deductible by the employer corporation, do require the ESOP trust to pay over such dividends to the employee-stockholder. The great flexibility usually available through varying the size of ESOP payments by the corporation into the trust, so long as credit contracts are met, makes this limitation of minor practical significance. Simultaneous ESOP financing of the corporation and of the employees' stock purchases is free from the risk that a capricious stock purchaser will himself interfere with the repayment of the ESOP loan financing. This is equally characteristic of each of the other six types of two-factor financing, again excepting RECOP financing.

Would-be home buyers are often denied access to credit because they do not meet certain arbitrary standards of creditworthiness or personal probity. In the case of RECOP financing, such considerations would have limited weight. For one thing, a down payment could be exacted if that were necessary to obtain commercial capital credit insurance for RECOP financing. (There should be a very compelling reason, however, to deviate from the general rule against self-insurance in capital financing.) Then, too, residential financing would unquestionably continue to be a mortgage-secured transaction. Finally, fierce attachment to the home is a characteristic human beings share with all territorial species. That in itself provides a high measure of security. Moreover, homeowners rarely fail to make their mortgage payments, and when default does occur, it is almost always because of the owner's deficient earning ability. But low earning power is caused primarily by our one-factor economic policy.

Debunking the Savings Mystique

The logic of democratic commercially insured capital credit financing eliminates institutional limits on the availability of capital credit, which are mythical except when based upon shortages of the physical ingredients necessary to production and consumption of goods and services. As costs are minimized through more efficient methods of finance, financing itself becomes increasingly more feasible. Rising incomes in the pockets of consumers who have the need and the desire to improve their material standard of living expands market demand for goods and services and thereby triggers increased production.

Technology tacitly but unequivocally promises an easier and more affluent life for those who are able to harness technological innovations in practical ways and thus raise their personal power to earn income and to consume and enjoy goods and services. Meanwhile, one-factor economists praise the virtues of renouncing consumption and advise would-be consumers to save instead of spend. These savings-mesmerized economists assure us that economic asceticism and deliberate suppression of mass consumption, upon which producers depend to stay in business, will eventually enable the dedicated underconsumer to realize the "American Dream" of capital ownership. But the reality is exactly the opposite. The American mind and our financing institutions need to be purged of the savings mystique, which prevents thinking about the economy in physical terms as a system. Understanding two-factor financing techniques and commercially insured capital credit would be important first steps in that direction.

Of course, some financial geniuses are able to parlay modest savings squeezed from labor income into large capital fortunes. This has been possible in every age. But rules that work for geniuses do not work for consumers in general, nor for the economy as a whole. Geniuses are, and always have been, in very short supply. Behind the phenomenon of the "self-made man" is a less obvious and more significant fact. The business genius tightens his belt only in the first stage of his quest for real capital riches. Not thrift but his ability to finance capital acquisition out of the wages of his capital is the secret of almost all of his impressive fortune.

The Relativity of Poverty over Time

As industry progresses, it becomes easier and easier to produce ever greater quantities of goods and services, often of improving quality. The socially acceptable level of subsistence and of a decent standard of living keep step with technology. The only permanent characteristic of affluence is its definition. *Affluence* means having enough income to buy what one considers to be a sufficiency of the things one needs and wants—having a *competence.*

Great personal and class differences exist between those who, because of their high capital-worker incomes, enjoy affluence and leisure and those who hold themselves above poverty only by increasingly frantic efforts and labors. Neither the economic nor the social nor the political implications of these qualitative differences can be minimized or disregarded merely because today's middle class may possess certain basic comforts that characterized an affluent standard of living at some point in the past. Nor is increasingly undemocratic distribution of economic power in the United States made less offensive by the fact that the poor manage to obtain, through coerced trickle-down and ignominious welfare, comforts that compare favorably with those enjoyed by the middle class of some bygone age.

In the distribution of social power, whether it be political power or economic power, all things are relative. The essence of economic democracy lies in the elimination of differences of earning power resulting from denial of equality of economic opportunity, particularly equal access to capital credit. Differences of economic status resulting from differences in advantages taken and uses made of economic opportunities are natural, proper, and desirable. But all differences based on inequality of economic opportunity, particularly those that give access to capital credit to the already capitalized and deny it to the non- or undercapitalized, are flagrant violations of the constitutional rights of citizens in a democracy.

When democratic finance becomes as easy as plutocratic finance, then a democratic nation will ensure that each capital financing is democratically structured. Businesses and individuals will not be permitted to further plutocratize our economy nor will they, once the economy is democratized, be permitted to resume their former practices. Simply put, savings-based financing tends toward plutocracy, while properly used and designed commercially insured capital credit financing tends toward democracy.

NOTES

1. Venture capital financing might continue to meet the first stage financing needs of new businesses.
2. CDRC is another name for the U.S. government. It is a reinsurance corporation backed only by the full faith and credit of the United States.
3. The logic behind the schematic for an economy operating on commercially insured capital credit rather than on savings financing was intuited by Harry

Scherman in *The Promises Men Live By* (New York: Random House, 1938). Scherman lacked two-factor economic insight, or he might have stumbled upon the ESOP and two-factor economics.

4. This is an estimate of the cost of operating what would amount to a highly computerized accounting system. The estimate is the ratio of the estimated clerical costs of operating the discount function of the Federal Reserve System spread over the estimated volume of capital financing transactions that would be discounted (monetized) through the system. We would expect that volume eventually to include virtually all nongovernmental capital financing.

5. Howard H. Baker, Jr., "Does the Congress Need Reform?" *San Francisco Chronicle,* April 18, 1984, p. A1.

CHAPTER 12

Democratizing the
Business Corporation

Lord, make all men feel that they are suffering from the
lack of my commodity. Let them not *really* need it,
since I would be uncharitable in asking that. Let them
just *think* they need it—and let them think so, very
very hard. And let them get the money somehow to
buy it.

Not from the government, since that would increase my
taxes. Not from higher wages, since that would increase my costs of production. And not as manna
from Heaven, since that would cause inflation.

All that I ask of Thee—Lord—is just one more miracle,
that good business shall not perish from the earth.
—"The Industrialist's Prayer"
Kenneth Burke, 1968

In the practical world, innovation usually comes before explanation. First the act, then the word. This was certainly true of the
business corporation. Over the centuries it evolved mainly by re-
sponding to specific economic stimuli. Its founders had no interest
in principle or theory nor concern for the long-term consequences
of corporate practices or policies. The business corporation therefore never developed theoretical models or plans that would enable
it to accommodate the more complex forms of enterprise imposed
on it by technological advance.

Despite its socially indifferent opportunism, however, the business corporation unquestionably remains one of humanity's greatest social inventions. It has an untapped, indeed unimagined,
potential for solving the very economic problems that defective
corporate strategy has done so much to create.

Once the Industrial Revolution had reached a point where the wealth of even the richest families was insufficient to finance the capital demands of enterprise, and the risks of loss were deemed too large for families or small groups of families to assume, an organization that could combine the components of industrial production with adequately limited liability became a necessity. Those components are:

- An employer having sufficient working capital and access to credit to pay wages and salaries reliably to the labor workers required
- A funding source for the land, structures, machines and capital intangibles—the physical or resource inputs—needed for each particular enterprise
- A means of limiting the liabilities of particular contributors to the organization to specifically invested capital and specifically assumed obligations
- A mechanism for using and managing the business components that would optimize the production and marketing of goods and services, finance continued growth, and allocate the income arising from production in a way acceptable to those who own and control the enterprise

Business corporations are legal entities created and sanctioned by law and custom to organize and carry on the production of goods and services that the private and public sectors consume or desire to consume. Well over a century of experience in the business community, in the state and federal legislatures, and in the judicial system have made it clear beyond doubt that business corporations now have almost all of the functional characteristics required to make them, in aggregate, the institutional building blocks of a democratic economy. Through them, all of the nation's economic activity, present or prospective, can be conducted rationally and satisfactorily.

The business corporation has, however, two outstanding shortcomings:

1. Although corporations are the dominant institution for the production and distribution of goods and services, under a one-factor, full-employment economic policy they cannot meet the requirement that the nation's economic institutions enable every consumer unit to participate in production (by

means consistent with current technology) to the extent necessary to earn enough income to support a reasonably acceptable lifestyle. A preindustrial, full-employment work opportunity does not satisfy this requirement, even if corporations were able to provide it, which they are not.

2. The domain of the business corporation has not been extended to include the broad, private ownership of all publicly used forms of capital. Thus the corporations have failed to harness a major part of the nation's capital stock that could provide millions of capital worker jobs for consumers, not to mention avoiding the high costs of crude one-factor public finance and the burdens imposed on taxpayers and consumers by public pension systems invested in low-yield, secondhand securities.

Corporate Economic Policy and National Economic Policy

As the basic building block in the economic system, the corporation should have a purpose that reinforces the national economic policy. The principal goal of a nation committed to a private-property, free-market democratic economy is the one Adam Smith identified in 1776. To be most efficient, and thus to make a maximum contribution to the growth of the wealth of the nation and the prosperity of its consumer-citizens, a nation should maintain a free-market economy, where the magic "invisible hand" identifies the nation's economic growth with the aggregate of the incomes of all the participants in production.[1] This motivates every household's breadwinners to do their best. The competition of producers in the marketplace keeps prices at a minimum and rewards producers who attract patronage by pleasing the customers most.

The purpose of production in a market economy is the consumption of goods and services by its own consumers. A close reading of *The Wealth of Nations* leaves no doubt that Smith meant consumption by the participants in production, and not just production targeted to meet vague goals without concern for how, why, or to whom that output is distributed.

A rational economic policy in a private-property, democratic market economy, then, must be centered on the individual consumer unit. It must include all individuals who are ready, willing, and able to participate in production in its current form. It must seek to optimize the quantity and quality of goods and services consumers want to buy, while exacting from them no more toil than current technology requires. It also must be democratic, assuring every individual or family a reasonable opportunity to take part in production and distribution.

The corporation must execute the national economic policy by optimizing the number of consumers who participate in production. In the United States, corporations produce about 90 percent of total goods and services.[2] They initiate and oversee most of the technological advances that replace labor work with capital work. Their executives are government's real economic advisers. Therefore, as a practical matter, they must also assume responsibility for providing their share of opportunities that assure every consumer unit its constitutional and natural right to participate in production concurrently as a labor worker and as a capital worker, thereby earning the income needed to support a reasonable standard of living and, in the process, the purchasing power to buy the economy's output.

Corporate Leadership in Deindustrializing America

Business corporations may also properly be held responsible for the deindustrialization of the U.S. economy that has taken place over the past half century. The turning point was 1932, when the "war on the effects of poverty" restored the nation's prosperity through national economic growth divorced from democratic economic growth of the earning power of the citizens; when we chose, in other words, a redistributive socialist solution rather than a democratic capitalist one.

At the corporate level, this policy shift involved the subtle conversion of the business corporation into a welfare machine. Managements joined with labor leaders and economists in propagandizing the consumers about the mystical "rising productivity of labor" that automation, attrition, and mergers pushed ever upward. This was the phenomenon that explained why working people were entitled to ever higher pay for ever diminishing work input, despite the fact that wages and salaries were determined not by market forces, but by bureaucrats through collective bargaining negotiations, "comparable pay," cost of living allowances, and other euphemisms for paying more because the consumers needed more.

Although it is primarily management that decides who and how many people will be employed as labor workers, and who and how many people shall participate in a business as capital workers, corporate management disavowed any responsibility for enabling consumers in general to earn more income so that they could buy the goods and services that corporations wanted to produce and sell. They eliminated labor worker jobs at every opportunity. Scientists, engineers, managers, and cost accountants were sought out for their cost-minimizing capabilities. At the same time, every effort was made through non-ESOP–structured mergers, acquisitions, leveraged buyouts, and corporate finance in general to concentrate more intensively the already concentrated ownership of capital and to divert the wages of capital into plutocratically owned economic growth.

The ESOP has been available to corporate managements for thirty years. Yet only about one in one hundred mergers, acquisitions, and leveraged buyouts is accomplished by this means; the remaining ninety-nine are plutocratic and do more to concentrate the ownership of corporate capital than their component corporate units have done under a defective national economic policy over the past half-century.

Aggressively Expanding the Domain of Private Business Corporations

Two-factor economic logic enables us to recognize that publicly used capital instruments—like sidewalks, streets, highways, transit systems, buildings, stadiums, ports, harbors, and parks—are capital instruments in precisely the same sense as are assets traditionally held in privately owned business corporations. Public use of these assets will be better served by putting them in the hands of people who are currently economically underpowered or whose labor worker employment would have to be coercively overpaid for them to earn an adequate income. Recapitalization of publicly held or used assets into privately owned ones will expand and democratize the private sector and, in the process, greatly expand the opportunities for lifetime employment for all consumers. At the same time, governmental entities would be gradually disengaged from the exercise of economic power. Not only would the cost burden on consumers and taxpayers be reduced, but the general public and employees—formerly public, now private—should take better care of capital assets in which they now have an economic interest. Symptoms of alienation, such as arson, vandalism, and carelessness, should be reduced, thus making public amenities less expensive to maintain and more conducive to civic pride. The massive costs to taxpayers of inadequate public pensions, the result of investment in low-yield secondary securities that benefit primarily Wall Street speculators, would also be eliminated. The ultimate result should be a renaissance in public improvements and amenities, as the capital infrastructure of the U.S. economy is restored by vigorous growth. A two-factor economic policy should prevent the new infrastructure from ever suffering the fate of the old one.

Policy Legislation for Democratized Capitalism

Unquestionably, a sound national economic policy is pivotal to sound corporate policy. Federal and state governments have the duty to adopt a sound economic policy. It is also government's duty to take primary responsibility for interpreting, administering, and enforcing the policy of redemocratizing economic power. Even though a few corporations, with significant help from Congress and some state legislatures, are beginning to use ESOPs, the dominant and accelerating trend within the U.S. economy today is still toward concentrating capital ownership into ever fewer hands. If we want to redemocratize economic power, we must do it through a new binary national economic policy.

Fortunately, the necessary policy legislation is already in place in the United States. Part of it will be found in the erroneously interpreted national economic policy law, which merely needs to be interpreted, applied, and enforced correctly. A key paragraph in Section 2 of the Employment Act of 1946 (15 U.S.C. 1021) refers to "employment" only in the conventional and traditional senses of the word. But that, of course, conflicts with the reality that an individual can participate in production and earn income not only by employing, or having others employ, his privately owned labor power, but also by employing, or having others employ, his privately owned capital.

Only about a dozen words in the act need to be changed or re-interpreted to correct this all-important policy declaration. Our suggestions are in bold type in the following paragraph that otherwise directly quotes the present law:

AMENDED DECLARATION OF POLICY

Section 2. The Congress hereby declares that it is the continuing policy and responsibility of the Federal Government to use all practicable means consistent with its needs and obligations and other essential considerations of national policy, with the assistance and cooperation of industry, agriculture, **banking, finance,** labor, and State and local governments, to coordinate and utilize all its plans, functions, and resources for the purpose of creating and maintaining, in a manner calculated to foster and promote free competitive enterprise and the general welfare, conditions under which there will be afforded useful employment opportunities, including self-employment, **as labor workers and as capital workers, for all consumers desiring economic autonomy and self-sufficiency,** and to promote maximum **concurrent** employment **as labor workers and capital workers, and** maximum production and purchasing power.

Work and *employment* are words that, rationally used, denote engaging in the production of goods and services and earning income as labor workers, as capital workers, or both. It is nonsense for us not to see that if there are two ways in which each individual can engage in production and earn income, then we must equally recognize as *work* both *labor work* and *capital work* that result in the production of useful and salable goods and services. And we must equally recognize as *employment* concurrent labor work and capital work, in any pragmatically sound combination.

The other part of the policy legislation under which we can begin to democratize the American economy is to be found in the common law of private property, which unambiguously asserts that the property rights of an owner do not include the right to use the thing owned in such way as to injure other human beings or their property. Nor do the rights of property entitle the owner to use his or her property in a manner that injures the public welfare.

These positive limitations are fortified by the American Constitution and by its prologue, the Declaration of Independence.

Lifetime Employment

One obvious implication of the fact that there are two ways to engage in production and earn income pertains to income after retirement. If we operate our institutions sensibly and properly and in accordance with the U.S. Constitution, people may, and indeed must, at the appropriate time, retire from the workaday labor world. But they should never retire from participation in production and earning income as capital workers. Labor work, by its very nature, is not and should not be a lifelong condition. Capital work, after its inception, should be. One's need for income continues to the end of life, and earning it legitimately in old age is just as important, both to the individual and to the economy, as legitimately supporting oneself and one's dependents through earlier years. If we are to discontinue the socialist experiment we have mistakenly undertaken since the 1930s and restore our economy to a private-property, free-market economic democracy, then lifetime employment should be everyone's personal economic goal, and all relevant institutions—governmental, business, and financial—should help families and individuals to achieve it.

There is a myth that Japanese workers receive "lifetime" jobs. The truth is that the largest Japanese employers, who *alone* have such arrangements, assure employment only to retirement age, which in most Japanese companies is fifty-five years of age. From age fifty-five to age sixty or sixty-five, when modest public pensions start, retired Japanese employees find themselves at an enormous disadvantage. Their public pensions, like all pensions, impose on them a radically reduced standard of living.

Capital Is Much More Productive Than It Appears

Can the democratization of capital ownership democratize economic power? We think that much of the answer to this question is to be found by determining the magnitude of the hidden productive power of capital as it becomes democratically owned by people who recognize its importance and assert their full property rights in it. Were the ownership of capital to be treated like the ownership of labor power—as a way to participate in production and earn income—it is clear that capital would be radically more productive than stockholders' income in today's economy would indicate. We estimate that, on the average, capital workers would earn substantially more than the 5 to 7 percent per annum yield they receive today from their equity stock portfolios.

First consider the nature and duration of the Industrial Revolution in the United States. It has been going on for over 200 years. Add the fact that the ability of the American economy to produce goods and services, while presently incalculable because of the statistical distortions of one-factor economics, is obviously hundreds of times greater, in per capita terms, than it was in colonial days. This difference is not primarily attributable to the input of labor workers, for thousands of skills have been destroyed compared with the modest number of new ones created by advanced technology. Our estimate is that 90 percent of total goods and services are now produced by capital workers and no more than 10 percent by labor workers, if the values of inputs and things produced are measured in hypothetical competitive market terms.

Figure 12–1 illustrates our estimate of the changing relative contributions of labor workers and capital workers to the value of goods and services produced by the American economy over the period of the Industrial Revolution.

Next let us consider the relatively quantifiable adjustments that could be made to reconstruct the productiveness of equity capital in the form of corporate assets owned, on paper, by stockholders. A typical corporation is in a 46 percent federal income tax bracket. Add to this an average 7 percent state corporate income tax levy that can be offset in part against the federal levy, and a federal levy of 7 percent of payroll for the employer's share of Social Security. A few major cities have municipal corporate income taxes as well. More than half the federal and state corporate income taxes and all of the employer's share of the Social Security tax are levied for the support of welfare. It is extremely conservative, therefore, to say that absent these taxes the potential return to stockholders would be doubled.[3]

Another quantifiable diversion of the earnings of capital away from stockholders is effected by corporate boards of directors. Since the redistributive innovations of the New Deal in the 1930s, directors are no longer compelled by our property laws, as they

Figure 12-1. Changing Participation of Labor and Capital Workers in Production of Goods and Services in the U.S. Economy.

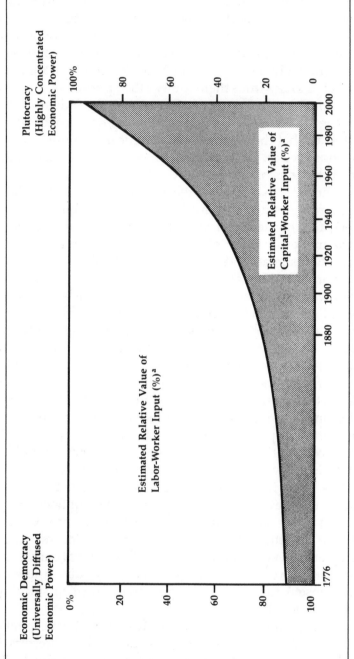

a. Estimated on the assumption that the value of productive inputs is measured in reasonably competitive markets.

were by common law, to pay the wages of capital to the owners of capital. Directors customarily "plow in" between half and three-fourths of the net after-tax earnings of corporations. This capital is retained in the corporation's own coffers to finance its growth and increase the concentration of ownership by its stockholders. In estimating the reduction in stockholders' earnings brought about by this method of financing growth, we must apply, on average, a factor of two to three to arrive at the increased earnings that would be distributed to stockholders in a democratized economy. Thus, the minimum increased productiveness of capital is in the range of four to six times greater than it appears to be.

Even this computation leaves out substantial nonquantifiable factors.

1. The goods and services produced by the economy contribute to the health of enterprise only if they are consumed through the market process. On an individual-by-individual basis, what each individual puts into the market economy through concurrent labor and capital work is accepted as the moral and legitimate basis for his or her income reward. Each participant in production, in market economic logic, is entitled to the fruit of his or her productive input.

But since 5 percent of the population owns substantially all of the nonresidential capital, and they and their corporations account for production of about 90 percent of the useful goods and services turned out annually by the economy, only a small part of the wages of their privately owned capital can be protected, or recognized, as income to them without causing an economic depression or breakdown. Every rhetorical and practicable expedient short of open repudiation of private property is used to keep the flow of consumer goods and services to the capitalless majority above the economic breakdown level.

One method for coercively diverting income away from the capital workers, who own the productive capital, to welfare recipients and to labor workers, who work with or benefit from it but do not own it, is the propagation of the myth of the "rising productivity of labor." It squeezes the property in capital and, at the resistance point,[4] passes on the remaining bloated labor costs to consumers and taxpayers. To numb the moral conviction that wealth belongs to those who create it, the dogma of the "rising productivity of labor" is repeated like an incantation. When the units of output of any particular enterprise are divided by the number of man-hours of input, "productivity" is said to go up, as relative hours of labor input go down. Rising "productivity" is then taken as the measure of an imaginary "increase" in labor's contribution to the productive process, so that as "productivity" goes up, wage demands are expected to, and avidly do, rise accordingly. Since there is a limit to how far the return to capital can fall without cutting off new capital formation entirely, this process redistributes only a limited portion of the wages of capital to the employees. The rest of such increases are absorbed by allowing production facilities to deteriorate and by passing them on to consumers and taxpayers as inflationary price increases. Although this resulting impairment of the return to capital workers is quite impossible to actually measure, it clearly takes a painful toll on the economic quality of life and on the health of the economy.

2. Another factor reducing the potential earnings of capital workers is the malicious destruction of capital assets that takes place year after year through arson, sabotage, and pilferage by the capitalless majority and by organized criminals of the underworld economy who are shut out from the legitimate economy by conventional finance and by one-factor corporate and national economic policies.

3. The productiveness of stock-represented capital assets is further impaired by the use of savings-based financing for capital transactions instead of commercially insured capital credit. Savings are costly, capriciously allocated, irrationally expensive (since interest rates are used to protect lenders against anticipated inflation, to which high interest rates are a main contributor), and always limited. Commercially insured capital credit would be relatively inexpensive because insurance premiums would be subject to competition, and the amount of such credit would be limited only by the physical ingredients available to be put into production and the resulting market demand of consumers with earnings to spend for useful goods and services.

4. The earnings of morbid capital—capital in excess of that which can or will be used to support the consumer lifestyles of the owners—are altogether diverted out of the market economy for useful goods and services. These earnings, instead, exacerbate economic imbalance by being used only to purchase additional morbid cap-

ital, the earnings of which will in turn be similarly sterilized for free-market purposes. Again, it is impossible to estimate the extent of this impairment of capital earning power, but it is significant.

5. Work rules that prevent the use of multiple work shifts in many capital-intensive industries are one of labor's prime means for slowing the erosion of jobs through technological change. The methods and pretexts are all too familiar: shift differentials, overtime limits and restrictions, hours of work traditions, convenience of supervisors, sheer coercion to increase jobs through featherbedding and other work rules, and so on. Capital in many industries, because of these impairments to its productiveness, becomes obsolete before it wears out. Many kinds of real capital, of course, already operate continuously, such as farms and rental structures. Oil, gas and mining operations, steel mills, aluminum pot lines, most chemical plants, ships, railroads, trucks, and other public utilities are normally kept running around the clock. But most of our capital stock is deliberately tied to the hours that suit the convenience of a one-shift labor force. In general, the labor force, backed by legislation, limits labor workers to working one six to eight hour shift per day for five days per week. This puts capital instruments out of operation from sixteen to eighteen hours per day for about 248 days per year, and entirely out of operation for some 104 days per year. To that must be added 30 to 45 days or more per employee for annual vacations, holidays, and "sick time," interpreted by many as leave they are entitled to take for domestic emergencies, personal business, or pleasure. In addition, there is the time lost each year to strikes and labor disputes. During the ten-year period 1971 through 1982, the average annual loss was 21 million man-workdays.[5] Another negative factor is employee "time theft" on the job, which personnel managers estimate at four to six and one-half hours per week per employee.

If real capital in our discontinuous industries were kept fully operating, with multiple shifts of labor and supervisors, there can be little doubt that its productiveness would be multiplied several times over. Nevertheless, it is a figure impossible, with present statistics, to quantify. We take no position on the desirability of conducting the economy so as to achieve the potentially higher productiveness of capital. We only point out that such intensification of capital output is theoretically possible.

The Effect of Simulfinancing on the True Productiveness of Capital

Simulfinancing—the simultaneous financing through two-factor constituency trusts of several desirable objectives with each single investment—is implicit in most of the two-factor tools for democratizing the economy. It has the effect of multiplying the productiveness of capital. A single investment can not only save federal and state corporate income taxes and Social Security taxes but, if used to purchase assets for the corporation, also generate an equal value of stock ownership for employees. What is more, two-factor financing methods, by adding to the lifetime capital worker employment of individuals, can eliminate wasteful redistributive efforts to bulwark their inadequate labor incomes through their employer's investment in low-yield, secondhand securities. Finally, because proper legislative implementation of two-factor financing concepts eliminates the individual's personal income taxation on funds used to buy capital and pay for it out of its own income, this, too, multiplies the productiveness of funds used for capital purposes.

We estimate that the productiveness of capital can be augmented another 100, 200, or 300 percent over and above the potential increments already noted. The general effect of these many forces that weaken the productiveness of capital in the current economy is to decimate it. Or to put the same thing in another way, capital in an economically democratized economy would be well over ten times more productive than we might suppose if we were only thinking in terms of the yields of secondhand stocks today. To illustrate the significance of this, let us suppose that a family today has an estate or holding of $500,000 of productive capital. If the leaks in the property pipeline that connect the owners with the full stream of the wages of capital were plugged, and a national and corporate economic policy of democratizing the economic power in the economy were fully implemented, then capital estates of about $50,000 would earn for their owners the same amount of income as does a half-million–dollar capital holding today.

There is another way to think about the significance of economic reforms that on the one hand would tighten up the laws of property so that stockholders would get the full yield of the assets represented by their stock, and on the other hand would make the acquisition of viable holdings of stock feasible for the average family. In September 1985 the National Center for Employee Ownership published its findings from a study of the ESOP experience of 145 companies over the period 1980–1984, showing the growth in participants' accounts over the five-year period and the projection of such accounts to 10, 20, and 30 years into the future. The following were the results at three salary levels:

- At a salary of $11,792 the stock value accumulated would be $20,370 after 10 years, $81,033 after 20 years, and $261,682 after 30 years.
- At a salary of $18,058 the stock value accumulated would be $31,195 after 10 years, $124,092 after 20 years, and $400,733 after 30 years.
- At a salary of $27,277 the stock value accumulated would be $47,121 after 10 years, $187,443 after 20 years, and $605,316 after 30 years.[6]

While we refrain from arguing that these projected amounts could be reliably multiplied by ten in each case if stockholders' property rights were fully restored and two-factor reforms adopted, it seems quite reasonable to assume that spectacular improvements in the average family's accumulation of wealth and spendable incomes would occur.

NOTES

1. This is Adam Smith's way of describing the marginal power of the freely competitive market where self-interest guides each participant in production to perform as if he were "led by an invisible hand to promote an end (the wealth of all) which was no part of his intention." Adam Smith, *The Wealth of Nations* (New York: Random House, 1937), p. 423.
2. In 1981, the latest date for which figures are available, total receipts of the 2,812,000 corporations doing business in the United States were 89.8 percent of the total receipts of all business enterprises. *Statistical Abstract of the United States* (Washington, D.C.: Bureau of the Census, 1985), Table 869, p. 516.
3. Over half of all federal and state taxes are levied on people who earn income to transfer that income to others who need more income. If democratizing two-factor efforts to raise the earnings of the economically underpowered were reasonably synchronized with those to eliminate the transfer taxes thereby made unnecessary, the economic feasibility of both measures would seem clear.
4. That this resistance point is misjudged in favor of maintaining the peace is evidenced in part by the widespread obsolescence of our public infrastructure

and our industrial productive facilities. We have granted more pay for less work, while ominously failing to keep our tools up to state-of-the-art levels.

5. *Statistical Abstract of the United States* (Washington, D.C.: Bureau of the Census, 1984), Table 730, p. 441.
6. Jonathan Feldman and Corey Rosen, *Employee Benefits in Employee Stock Ownership Plans: How Does the Average Worker Fare?* (Arlington, Virg.: National Center for Employee Ownership, September 1985).

PART III

UNIONS' NEW ROLE

CHAPTER 13

The Unions' Role in Democratizing Capitalism

The greatest task before civilization at present is to make machines what they ought to be, the slaves, instead of the masters of men.

—*Havelock Ellis, 1921*

The American labor union is ideally qualified to champion the cause of democratizing economic power in every respect but one—it has encumbered itself with a basic wrong idea. Ironically, this wrong idea is the emotional heart of labor union ideology, as well as the premise of the national economic policy of full (labor worker) employment that was already an anachronism at the time it was formally adopted, at organized labor's insistence, in 1946.

The unions' error is simply the one we hope we have exposed and corrected in this book: the belief that labor work is the only way to participate in production and earn income and the related belief that capital mystically amplifies the "productivity" (implying productiveness) of workers who own no interest in it. Implicit in this thinking is the idea that it makes no difference who owns the capital, as long as there is plenty of it available.

This mistaken analysis of the economic facts of life has sabotaged the trade union movement since its inception in nineteenth-century Britain. On the one hand, unions have recognized and fought against the economic injustice wreaked by technological progress in lowering the incomes of working people. On the other hand, they have been forced to wage this just war with self-defeating and morally questionable weapons. Chief among these has been a form of terrorism, actual or threatened, used to coerce the employer to grant employees for whom they bargain progressively more pay than would be accorded by the competitive free market for progressively less work input. In short, a misunderstanding of the changing nature of production led trade unions, increasingly with government assistance, gradually to convert productive enterprises in the private and public sectors of the American economy into welfare institutions.

U.S. labor unions, which have so powerfully influenced legislation aimed at raising the incomes of working people and at achieving social welfare goals, were heavily influenced by the writings of the European evolutionary socialists of the eighteenth and nineteenth centuries, just as America's political founders took their basic ideas from the works of the European political philosophers of that period.

The inspiration for those socialist beginnings was, of course, the devastating poverty and unbearable social conditions engendered by the first shocks of the Industrial Revolution and the accompanying urbanization of England and Europe from the middle of the eighteenth century on. The leading philosophers of the socialist movement[1] fixed the terms of the controversy between the conventions and laws of private property in capital assets, on the one hand, and the claims of people who own only their labor power—their power to work—on the other. Thomas Malthus spoke for the propertied and their supporters in the Church, the universities, and the courts:

A man who is born into a world already possessed, if he cannot get subsistence from his parents on whom he has a just demand, and if the society do not want his labour, has no claim of *right* to the smallest portion of food, and, in fact, has no business to be where he is. At Nature's mighty feast there is no vacant cover for him. She tells him to be gone, and will quickly execute her own orders.[2]

The propertyless not unnaturally responded by repudiating an institution that denied even their right to live, if it conflicted with the interests of the property holder. They elevated the productive importance of their labor power, their sole source of economic power. Building on the ideas of the earlier English socialists, the Gotha Programme of the German socialists in 1875 laid down as a fundamental principle that

labour is the source of all wealth and all civilisation, and that generally beneficial labour being only possible through society, *the whole produce of labour belongs to society:* that is to say, *that, work being universally compul-*

sory, every member of society has an equal right to a share of the product according to his reasonable requirements.[3]

None of the scholars who forged the socialist tradition seems to have come to grips with the possibility, first envisioned by Aristotle, that if production instruments (tools) should ever become able to accomplish their own work, obeying or anticipating the will of their masters, "...if the shuttle could weave and the plectrum touch the lyre without a hand to guide them, chief workmen would not want servants, nor masters slaves."[4] Aristotle clearly saw that if self-acting machines ever were invented, their owners would produce goods and services through them and that human labor, then enslaved, could be liberated.

Throughout history when labor was (or at least seemed to be) the dominant source of productive input, the error of assuming there is but one way for people to participate in production and to earn income, when in fact there are two, did not seriously frustrate the operation of a market economy. To be sure, without labor workers, capital workers could produce very little—perhaps nothing—except in the case of landowners who grew wild fruit trees in benign climates. But as industrialization proceeded, it became equally true that without capital workers and their productive assets, most of the goods and services produced by modern economies would be impossible to produce. Workers cannot carry people or cargo across bodies of water, nor fly passengers or freight through the air, nor drill oil wells or offshore oil wells, nor fabricate metal, nor mine ores in significant quantities, nor produce chemicals, nor take x-ray pictures, nor, indeed, produce affluent levels of goods and services in general.

Labor's Impossible Dream

Labor unions in the United States, from their mid-nineteenth century beginning, accepted the ideas of the eighteenth- and nineteenth-century English and European socialists that the laws and conventions of private property necessarily imposed hardship upon those who had no way to earn income but to sell their labor power in markets where technological advance steadily eroded demand for labor.

No moral principle is more widely accepted, however, than that of free-market morality: Individuals should not demand progressively more pay for the same or a reduced work input *in the absence of free-market forces* heightening demand for labor. But the working community also believes that as long as a man or woman is doing a good job, his or her real income should steadily rise. This persistent promise of a better and easier life has been inspired by the unfolding technology that has made the production of goods and services ever more abundant and effortless. Against the background of American democracy, it was inevitable that trade unions should expect their members' incomes to rise so as to enable them to participate in the nation's spectacular economic growth and progress as consumers. Nevertheless, labor unions took on an impossible task, especially in the United States. They had to reconcile their members' rising expectations with simple free-market morality, while adhering to the socialist formula that only labor produces goods and services in a nation more fiercely committed to the institution of private property than any in Europe.

To justify their bargaining demands, the trade union leaders persuaded society to accept, or pretend to accept, the myth of the "rising productivity of labor." Instead of maintaining with Karl Marx that the rising profits of employers, in the face of diminishing demand for labor, proved that after a certain number of technological generations capital produces spontaneously like the sun, they attributed rising output to labor and demanded higher compensation.

All honor is due to the early socialists who first had the imagination and courage to see and proclaim the inherent promise of technology to produce general affluence and to formulate a more just and humane society. They were correct in their belief that material scarcity and the suffering, exploitation, and social conflict that scarcity fostered were capable of being abolished by a wise use of technology. They were the first to question the inevitability of poverty, brute ignorance, and war; to challenge tyranny, unbridled industrial greed, and selfish nationalism.

The industrially inspired vision of the ever rising economic quality of life, first seen and pressed upon society by the socialist evolutionary philosophers, and coercively translated into action by welfare and labor legislation and the stepped-up activities of the labor unions over the past sixty years, not only can be realized – its realization is in fact long overdue. Labor unions can play the part they have always aspired to in this desperately needed transition. But first they must adopt a sound strategy that conforms to the economic facts of life. If under free-market conditions, 90 percent of the goods and services are produced by capital input, then 90 percent of the earnings of working people must flow to them as wages of their capital and the remainder as wages of their labor work. We have already demonstrated that this is feasible. Indeed, we believe that it is inevitable. The question is only whether the labor union will help lead this movement or, refusing to learn, to change, and to innovate, become irrelevant.

The lesson of two-factor economics is that the political and economic salvation of the capitalless majority lies in the extension and enforcement of the laws and institutions of private property, and not in their overthrow or further erosion by socialist-inspired redistribution, which Americans are currently repudiating. Organized labor has an unprecedented opportunity – a second chance – to fulfill its destiny.

Labor unions must reformulate themselves into *producers'* unions representing members who are concurrently labor workers and capital workers; people whose property rights in both factors must be equally protected; people who regard the job of producing goods and services not as economic civil war between labor workers and capital workers, or even between shop workers and management workers, but as a peaceable cooperative activity to be carried on through the two agents that should be owned by everyone who wants to be a consumer. A new generation of labor leaders must steer organized labor in this new direction. Rather than seeking higher pay and fringe benefits in ways that assure those gains will be lost in higher consumer prices, rising taxes, diminished affluence, adverse trade balances, and vanishing freedom and democracy, leaders of the new producers' unions must gain their leadership in ways whereby their constituents, and indeed the society, gain as producers, gain in freedom from redistributive taxes, and gain by combining economic autonomy with political democracy to forge again a truly democratic society.

By taking up this challenge, labor unions will broaden their functions, revitalize their constituency, and spectacularly reverse their decline.

NOTES

1. See Anton Menger, *The Right to the Whole Produce of Labour* (London: McMillan & Co., Ltd., 1899; reprint ed., New York: Augustus M. Kelley, 1970). These were William Godwin (England, 1756–1836), Charles Hall (England, c. 1745–

1825), William Thompson (England, c. 1783–1833), Claude Henri de Rouvroy Saint-Simon (France, 1760–1825), Robert Owen (Scotland, 1771–1858), Pierre-Joseph Proudhon (France, 1809–1865), Karl Johann Rodbertus (Germany, 1805–1875), Karl Marx (Germany, 1818–1883), Louis Blanc (France, 1811–1882), and Ferdinand Lassalle (France, 1825–1864).

2. Ibid., p. 4. Menger notes that this famous passage, which appeared in the second edition of Malthus' *An Essay on the Principle of Population* published in 1803, was omitted by Malthus in the third edition of 1806 and in later editions.

3. Ibid., p. 107.

4. Aristotle, *Politics*, Book I, Chapter 4. See Louis O. Kelso and Mortimer J. Adler, *The Capitalist Manifesto* (New York: Random House, 1958), p. 26.

CHAPTER 14

Do Labor Unions Have a Future?

For every $5,000 worth of investment, you can get rid of
one worker. The machine has no vacations, no pensions,
no fringe benefits.
— *An AFL-CIO Official, 1963*

"I think a lot of people think unions have outlived their usefulness," said Richard L. Lesher, president of the Chamber of Commerce of the United States. Indeed, unions are on the defensive.
Union membership has declined steadily for thirty years to about
20 percent of the labor force today. Unions are unable to organize
new members to replace those lost. Before 1974 they invariably
won more than half the representation elections in every year. But
since 1974 their winning percentage has dropped year by year to
44 percent of the 4,320 elections held in 1982. Even where unions
have won the right to bargain, an AFL-CIO study shows that five
years after workers have voted for a union, one-third of the elections have not resulted in a signed contract. In the 1970s decertification elections to eliminate a union within a business were
rare. Today they are on the rise and are successful in three tries
out of four. In 1982, 682 groups of workers voted to decertify their
unions.[1]

The election of the Reagan administration in 1980 and the
smashing reaffirmation of the Republican position in 1984 reflect
the ability of a large proportion of voters to discern a direct relationship between progressively higher pay for the same or diminished work input and an economy sinking into a recession visible
to everyone except the contending politicians.

These signs of growing labor union weakness have cost organized labor both pay and benefits concessions. Wage increases in
major contracts in 1983 were the lowest that they have been in the
sixteen years that the Labor Department has been documenting

them. Gains from collective bargaining throughout the economy have not only peaked, but "concessionary reductions" in wages and benefits are now being made in industries and businesses across the board. Strikes have become less effective as bargaining tools. The 1980s saw fewer strikes than has any decade since World War II. Employers are more willing to resist strikes, even to the extent of closing plants and stores. Management attitudes are toughening, and setbacks for unions are the order of the day. Both sides of the bargaining table recognize that the National Labor Relations Board, which prior to 1980 was dominated by board members eager to help labor gain more income, now reflects a change in attitude emanating from President Reagan's appointments to the board.

Even Lane Kirkland, president of the AFL-CIO, has speculated that the elimination of major portions of existing labor law might be a good thing. Behind his words is the hope that active cooperation between several unions, now illegal as "secondary boycotts," might bring management to its knees. Clearly this betrays an extreme degree of economic frustration, for Kirkland well knows that should labor succeed in packing its wages with more welfare, American producers will be further set back and foreign competitors encouraged. Thomas R. Donahue, secretary-treasurer of the AFL-CIO, looks for a solution in an "industrial policy," under which the inadequate and shrinking market value for labor would be offset by government regulation, government subsidies, intensified redistribution, and synthesized work.[2]

But there are signs that the labor unions' unused collective bargaining weapon—bargaining for the right to earn income as capital workers through the use of the ESOP and bargaining to buy for employees corporations and corporate assets that are for sale or in action—will soon be unsheathed. Only that solution addresses itself to all of the ills in ways that ensure that employees, consumers, managements, shareholders, and owners—indeed all Americans—gain.

Freeing Producers' Unions from One-Factor Economics

By accepting the myth of the rising productivity of labor and using it to achieve the goal that Samuel Gompers (founder of the American labor movement) so tersely summarized as "more," the trade unions have directed the labor movement down an economic, political, and ideological dead-end street. Higher wages for less work input may look like "more" in the short run, but the fundamental immorality of the idea (once the erroneous assumption is exposed), the resulting inflation, and the impact of continuing technological change eventually convert the illusory gains into less: less real income after inflation, less overall production of goods and services for the economy as a whole, less income-earning security, less permanent (non-lifetime) employment, less economic freedom from subsistence toil, less political freedom, less economic opportunity, and less moral credibility.

Because they live on the cutting edge of economic reality, labor leaders and their constituents are all too painfully aware that the productiveness of labor is in fact declining. They know that the dominant factor of industrial production in all industrialized economies is capital. The person who works through capital can in general produce more—often ridiculously more—and earn more than the person who works only through labor.

At a 1940 congressional hearing where one labor representative repeated the official labor position that "machines are but *instruments* for the *multiplication* of manpower,"[3] another labor leader voiced a different interpretation:

I heard over the radio only Saturday a man speaking on behalf of the rural-electrification program, who said a farmer for a nickel could buy enough kilowatts to equal a full day's labor of a man, so that on that basis human labor is reduced to 5 cents a day. Now, if we are going to listen to the arguments that capital efficiency brought about this efficiency, that labor didn't bring this about, that labor should be paid what it is worth but no more, on that standard a farm laborer would be worth 5 cents a day.[4]

This plain-speaking man was Byrl Whitney, then director of education and research of the Brotherhood of Railroad Trainmen. He also said: "I am condemning the social conscience which builds up these mechanisms designed to offset the economic cheapness of human labor, the change from the days of the wilderness, when probably all economic production was 95 percent human labor, to now, when it is 2 or 3 percent human labor."[5]

Thirty years later, an international trade union official and economist, to illustrate the magnitude of the automation revolution, cited a United Nations estimate that "over 80 percent of increases in gross national product is today contributed by technological progress and capital." The U.N. report further estimated that in the United States and Sweden, where average wages and living standards are the highest in the world, the contribution of labor is estimated at only 10 percent of GNP. Technology and capital account for 90 percent.[6]

To extricate the twentieth-century labor union from the ideological dead-end where history delivered it, let us acknowledge that plutocratic capitalism, with its one-factor perspective, gave working people no other alternative but to band together to wage war on the law of supply and demand as it applied to the price of labor and on private property in capital. Samuel Gompers had to look no further than his own experience as a cigar maker. "In my trade, the workmen were powerless against the substitution of machines for human skill. Regularly we suffered annual reduction in wages. . . we needed protection desperately."[7] Let us further acknowledge that a society that pits fragile human labor against the tireless power of the machine and the boundless energy in matter is as primitive and cruel as those societies that once, for sport, pitted men against the fiercest beasts in deadly combat. By combining these two conditions with financing methods that limit access to capital credit to the already rich, thus excluding the working class, we perpetrate the most flagrant denial of equal protection of the laws and equal privileges and immunities to the workers, while taking (diminishing the value of) their property in their labor power for public purposes, without giving them constitutional due process.

The myth of the rising productivity of labor filled a conceptual vacuum created by one-factor economics. But this myth has redounded upon the twentieth-century labor union with a vengeance. Under its cover, the capital owner has continued to accumulate the ownership of productive capital that would be the real source of industrial prosperity and power if it were democratically owned. Indeed, circumstantial evidence suggests that there has been a tacit but conscious accommodation between organized labor and corporate management, for their misunderstood mutual benefit, to transfer income from consumers and taxpayers to themselves. Labor unions, it seems, would not make an issue of concentrated capital ownership as long as managements would redistribute much of the wages of capital to labor, load the rest of labor's and management's rising earnings on consumers and taxpayers, and maintain strict, if mysterious, silence about labor's and management's dwindling productive roles.

The twentieth-century labor union has inherited strategies and mechanisms that once helped wrest a portion of the wages of capital from the concentrated owners but now impede the formulation of a new producers' leadership role conforming on the one hand to the facts of modern production and distribution and on the other to the dependence of economic production upon vigorous consumer power and humanity's universal longing to live better. Labor's outgrown legacy includes the psychology of *We vs. Them* — glorifying the confrontation between capital and labor (or their representatives), while denigrating knowledge of business operation and corporate finance as the traditional domain of "them," where propertyless labor trespasses as an outsider.

If there are in reality two ways for people to participate in production and earn income, then tomorrow's producers' union must take cognizance of both. The worker's economic problem is to earn, by engaging in production, enough income to afford the lifestyle he reasonably chooses for himself and his family. It is both easier and more pleasant to produce that income through one's privately owned capital than it is to suffer the strife, frustration, impairment of production, and inflation brought on by resorting to coercive union power and legislation to redistribute an increasing part of the incomes of consumers, taxpayers, and capital workers. Since many kinds of work are not only monotonous and disagreeable but hazardous to longevity and health, and since the object of economic activity is not more toil but more affluence and leisure, clearly the greater the ability of individuals and families to earn their incomes as capital workers, the better. The important thing is to achieve productive autonomy for all people without coercion of consumers and taxpayers, and without inflation.

Testifying before the Joint Economic Committee of Congress in 1967, Walter Reuther, president of the United Auto Workers, expressed the opinion that stock distributions to workers "would help to democratize the ownership of America's vast corporate wealth which is today appallingly undemocratic and unhealthy."

If workers had definite assurance of equitable shares in the profits of the corporations that employ them, they would see less need to seek an equitable balance between their gains and soaring profits through augmented increases in basic wage rates. This would be a desirable result from the standpoint of stabilization policy because profit sharing does not increase costs. Since profits are a residual, after all costs have been met, and since their size is not determinable until after customers have paid the prices charged for the firm's products, profit sharing [in the form of stock distribution to workers] cannot be said to have any inflationary impact upon costs and prices.[8]

Had his life not been cut short, Walter Reuther could well have been the first labor leader of an industrial union to understand the logic of democratizing economic power and to implement its capital-ownership-broadening techniques in factories employing members of the United Auto Workers.

There is a lesson here for producers' union leaders as well as for political leaders. To paraphrase George Meany, who thought foreign policy "too damn important to be left to the Secretary of State," universal economic autonomy through democratizing capitalism is much too important a subject to be left to the entrenched one-factor economists.[9] A great educational task awaits a nation that decides to economically enfranchise not only its labor force but all its economic underproducers through private ownership of productive capital. Producers' unions must take on a large part of that responsibility. Fortunately, they have the incipient organizations already in place.

Millions of workers throughout the Western capitalist bloc are already rejecting political and union supervision of their work lives and living standards because they sense that unionism represents not peaceful economic power but coercive power. The same passion for freedom and independence is making totalitarian institutions increasingly unworkable in the anticapitalist Marxian bloc.

The Costs of Labor's One-Factor Gains

The achievements of a century of trade unionism in the United States, particularly in the last half of that century, during which the economic policies and powers of federal and state governments aggressively supported the unions, have been real. But it is equally self-evident that the price of these gains has been very high and is growing, and that this system does not work satisfactorily. The unions that have succeeded in coercing the highest wages have most severely crippled the industries that employ them: automobile manufacturing, steel manufacturing and fabrication, railroading, shipping, house building, air transportation, radio manufacturing, television manufacturing, agricultural implement manufacturing, heavy machinery production, and so forth. With negligible exceptions, even the ultimate test of success in a plutocratic capitalist economy—how much capital ownership one has accumulated—has been failed by working people.

Working conditions for the labor force have, of course, improved over the years. But the economic quality of life for the majority of Americans has trailed far behind the technical capabilities of the economy to produce creature comforts, and even further behind the desires of consumers to live economically better lives. The missing link is that most of those unproduced goods and services can be produced only through capital, and the people who need them have no opportunity to earn income from capital ownership.

Inflation over the past fifty years destroyed three-fourths of the purchasing power of the dollar. The mere plateauing of the *rate of inflation* does not prevent the cost of goods and services from being bloated with welfare and inflation. The success of the Reagan administration in repressing inflation through unemployment, budget deficits, and trade deficits is destined to be short lived. Technological change, which diminishes the demand for jobs and increases the supply of unemployed workers, marches relentlessly forward, and the only change that could accommodate it successfully—the adoption and vigorous implementation of a policy of democratizing capital ownership—is as yet nowhere in sight.

In the past, the constant growth in the size and strength of labor unions along with their audacious demands for increased compensation in return for diminished labor input has been the main cause of the corporate merger movement, just as the reverse is true. Where the force employed is coercion, bigness is required to cope with bigness in a brute power struggle. Autonomy, that cherished quality of a free and democratic society, is stifled in the course of this struggle.

Liberal education, which should steadily become a more basic and pervasive influence in the lives of free citizens as more of the toil is shifted from our shoulders and borne by capital instruments, is being crowded out by the demands for vocational education, required to qualify the individual for synthesized and subsidized jobs.

As technology advances and the elite few capital workers take over more and more of the production of our goods and services, the absurdity of an ever growing proportion of the population engaging in "jobs" becomes apparent. With 95 percent of Americans having nothing to sell in the economy except their labor work, the quality of their lives continues to erode from a psychic malady we call *economic alienation.* Economic alienation is an awareness, up to now generally unarticulated, that the productive activity of society can proceed without one's self; that the individual has been robbed of the economic virility through which he could *produce* in proportion to his desire to consume; that his economic impotence is being concealed by artificially contrived "jobs" rather than being cured by institutional changes that would restore economic democracy as technology shifts the burden of production from labor to capital workers. This, we submit, is the real basis of the alienation of today's youth throughout the world. They are being ushered into a world where – in this critical and basic economic sense – they are not and will not be needed, except to make war or engage in some other form of synthesized make-work.[10]

The union movement, through both its sins of commission and omission, has been a prime factor in bringing about the concentration of the ownership of capital. It has sought to protect the ideologically postulated rising productive power of its members' labor rather than their *right to be competitively productive* in ways that reflect the state of the productive arts. In so doing, it has failed to demand for its members equality of economic opportunity in the form of equal and effective opportunity to acquire ownership of capital. More ominously, because the union movement, in order to secure a better standard of living for its members, has been forced to assert the increasing productiveness of labor *where there is none*, it has fallen victim to a correspondingly erroneous strategy on the part of corporate management and management of the financial institutions. These are the techniques of conventional finance that channel the growth of capital ownership, stunted though it may be, into the small percentage of households that already own it all.

"Job security" measures, like those attained in 1984 bargaining by the United Auto Workers, are mere replications of the shortsighted practice of unions to protect their older membership against competition from those who seek employment. Attrition tactics have been widely employed by unions and managements throughout the past half century to throw the burden of unemployment on the young.

The democratizing of capitalism converts *more* based upon redistribution into *more* based upon increased production and increased earning power. Thus, ESOPs and other two-factor financing techniques do not change the ancient goal of labor; they legitimate it. But they do much more. Redistribution merely restructures the means of sharing in the output of a finite economy. It converts excess affluence of some into increased subsistence for others. Democratizing capitalism and the tools for implementing a two-factor economic policy, however, not only protect the ownership of those who presently own capital, but make capital workers of those who do not, thus raising their earning power and the productive power of the economy.

NOTES

1. All statistics in this paragraph are from the *New York Times*, September 3, 1984, p. 1.
2. Ibid.
3. U.S., Congress, Temporary National Economic Committee, *Investigation of Concentration of Economic Power, Hearings before the Temporary National Economic Committee pursuant to Public Resolution No. 113*. 75th Cong., 3rd sess., April 1940, pp. 16731–32. In a sense, of course, the statement would be true if we were talking about the "manpower" of the capital owner.
4. Ibid., p. 16911.
5. Ibid., p. 16916. The Brotherhood of Railroad Trainmen still exists today, but the proud industry it represents is mostly socialized—a victim of society's failure to find sound ways to reconcile people to technology. Court-appointed trustees and lawyers, representing the rich shareholders, bondholders, and grasping managements, plunder its valuable real estate properties and sell off its historical buildings and artifacts to restaurant chains.
6. Charles Levinson, *Capital, Inflation and the Multinationals* (New York: Macmillan, 1971), p. 51.
7. Samuel Gompers, *Seventy Years of Life and Labor*, Vol. 1 (New York: E.P. Dutton & Company, 1925), p. 50.
8. U.S., Congress, Joint Economic Committee, *Economic Report of the President, Hearings before the Joint Economic Committee*. 90th Cong., 1st sess., February 1967, pt. 4., p. 774.
9. *New York Times*, August 19, 1975, p. 31. Meany was paraphrasing the remark attributed to Talleyrand that war is much too serious to be left to the generals.
10. See Richard L. Rubenstein, *The Cunning of History* (New York: Harper & Row, 1975).

CHAPTER 15

The ESOP: Prime Tool for the New Producers' Unions

Productive property owned in undivided shares by laboring men, contention over the division of products replaced by general fraternity—this is the ideal which humanity has repeatedly approached, abandoned, and approached again.

—John Bates Clark, 1885

While the logic of two-factor and free-market economics is immutable, applying the ESOP concept to specific corporations within that theoretical framework is a complex investment banking art. No two businesses are alike, and existing ESOP laws and regulations leave considerable room for variations in design. The first step, then, that producers' unions at the international level should take to become more effective in representing their members under a democratizing ownership strategy is to learn as much as they can about two-factor financing technology. Only knowledge will prepare them to advise their local unions on the qualifications of investment bankers, financial lawyers, labor lawyers, accounting and valuation firms, and other necessary technical specialists.

Traditionally, the costs of professional advice used by companies are borne by the companies themselves. Without interfering with this arrangement, producers' unions should assure that the advantages of simulfinancing—the generation of capital ownership in employees concurrent with the solving of businesses' own capital financing problems—are obtained in every capital financing transaction. To ensure that qualified ESOP investment bankers and other necessary experts are chosen, producers' unions might have to employ their own experts and have a voice in the selection of consultants. How those costs are ultimately borne between employer and employees and the producers' unions representing employees is, of course, a matter for collective bargaining. Once precedents are established, such details should be disposed of in a minimum of time.

The overall strategy of producers' unions should assure, so far as possible, that the labor compensation of its members does not exceed the labor costs of the employer's competitors, and that capital earnings of its members are built up to a level that optimizes their combined labor-capital worker earnings. In other words, the goal is to minimize the toil and maximize the earnings and leisure of each member, to the extent consistent with competitively producing goods and services of the highest quality.

Acquiring Ownership through ESOP Financing

Most of the stock in publicly held corporations is owned by institutional speculators who buy the shares, hold them for capital gains, and then sell, using the proceeds to acquire new securities. Approximately 85 percent of the trading in publicly held securities is by financial intermediaries, predominantly pension funds.[1] A move to acquire ownership or even control of such corporations generally triggers sizable speculator profits. This occurs because stock market trading in secondhand securities normally values stocks at prices well below the per-share market value of the corporations themselves *as going concerns*. Speculators are usually pleased when a legitimate and capable buyer wants to purchase an enterprise in which they hold shares.

In most corporations, the moment that management (often meaning the chief executive officer and a few other top executives) decides that an acquisition either of control or of all of the stock of the corporation is a good idea, or one that cannot successfully be resisted, the corporation is in play. In every practical sense it is for sale, voluntarily or otherwise. A sale almost always requires approval of the corporation's stockholders; sometimes by a mere majority, sometimes by two-thirds or more of the voting stock, depending upon the corporate charter and upon the laws of the incorporating state.

Any publicly held corporation put up for sale by those who speculate in its stock is almost invariably a potential candidate for purchase through ESOP financing by its natural shareholders—

its employees. A change, or a seriously threatened change, in ownership or control should provide grounds for reopening any labor contract covering any of the corporation's employees under the guidance of competent union executives and labor lawyers. The union can then demand mandatory collective bargaining over the purchase of the business on behalf of *all* employees of the corporation at the same price that any independent buyer would pay.

Early in the proceedings the union should retain qualified ESOP investment bankers to advise it on the economic feasibility and proper design of an ESOP acquisition and on the steps required to finance and execute the transaction. At the outset the union should determine from the most reliable information it can obtain, including key employees of the corporation, whether the corporation's management is adequately qualified to lead the firm after it becomes employee owned. It should also find out whether management is motivated to join in the ESOP acquisition and on what mutually acceptable terms.

More often than not, the competing potential buyer or buyer group will have offered a few key managers the opportunity to acquire stock in the new acquisition corporation on very favorable terms. Experience shows that after outside acquisition, few if any executives fare as well or encounter such fascinating and potentially rewarding challenges as the executives who join with their fellow employees to buy the corporation through an ESOP. Indeed, large numbers of middle managers have no future at all when the company is bought or merged through a plutocratic leveraged buyout. They are fired, and often top management gets the boot as well. Absent legislation that would make a democratizing ESOP buyout decisively more attractive than any other buyout, common bargaining sense dictates that reasonable key-man perquisites offered by the outside non-ESOP buyer should be matched by whatever additional key-man stock arrangements are needed to make the ESOP's offer competitive to the executives. Of course, an enlightened executive will realize that he or she is negotiating with a producers' union whose membership may soon include all corporate employees should the ESOP acquisition prove successful. Management in that case will be addressing future fellow shareholders as well as employees, although nothing in the contemplated ESOP buyout would, in and of itself, diminish their status as managers. The ESOP acquisition merely transforms a prior adversarial relationship into a cooperative relation-ship—a new solidarity—between people who are all owners and producers.

If the union's proposal does not proceed smoothly to acquisition bargaining and closing of the ESOP purchase, the union should consider filing in the appropriate Federal District Court a class action suit on behalf of all employees of the corporation seeking an injunction against acquisition or control of the corporation by any non-ESOP buyer. This would give the union time, say, three to six months, to negotiate and close the purchase of the company by its employees through an ESOP. If necessary, unions should plan in advance to seek congressional recognition of their right to such injunctive relief.

If there are already several unions representing various groups of corporate employees, a labor council should be organized to resolve quickly the joint representation problems, both intermediate and long-term. All reasonable union expenses incurred by such activities should be recognized by the U.S. Departments of Treasury and Labor, which have regulatory jurisdiction over ESOPs, as proper costs to be borne by the ESOP and paid out of the purchase financing at the acquisition's close.

Saving Capital-Worker Jobs from Emigration

The union has an even stronger case for federal court assistance when the potential buyer is foreign. A foreign acquisition exports all of the capital-worker jobs permanently out of the economy, even if the labor worker jobs remain. Since an ESOP could make all of the target corporation's work force capital workers, the capital worker opportunity loss is almost always larger than that represented by existing U.S. shareholders. The 1984 acquisition of Carnation Corporation, headquartered in Los Angeles, by Nestle S.A. of Vervey, Switzerland, and the purchase of U.S. Industries by the Hanson Trust of Great Britain during that same year are just two examples of the capture by foreign corporations of over 18,000 potential capital worker positions from the U.S. economy. Every such foreign investment contributes to the unemployment of potential capital workers in the United States. Unfortunately, this job drain is neither identifiable nor correctable under our defective one-factor economic policy.

What has been said of public corporations ordinarily and chiefly owned by speculators applies equally to closely held but privately owned corporations whose owners (individual or corporate) or managers indicate that they intend to sell ownership or control to any buyer other than an ESOP for its employees. Such a transaction is illustrated by the Searle family, holders of about 34 percent of the stock of G. D. Searle & Co. of Skokie, Illinois, which asked management to seek a buyer for the company for an indicated value of $2.8 billion.[2] G.D. Searle was thereafter sold to Monsanto Company, thus preventing 7,000 employees from embarking upon capital worker careers and bulwarking their wages or salaries with capital earnings. Dozens upon dozens of giant corporations are in this posture at any particular moment.

Implementing Earnings Planning for Union Members

The ESOP and other two-factor financing techniques can enable unions to take the lead in bringing the capital wages of their members into line with the state-of-the-art technology for similar corporations. Unions then have a means of averting the damage done to business and industry, and to competitiveness in general, by pressing for wage levels that make the businesses uncompetitive.

Using a two-factor collective bargaining strategy, the producers' unions can be as sensitive as management to the competitive facts of life. If maximizing automation gives an employer corporation a competitive advantage, then the internal response should be to bargain for ESOP financing that will cause a larger share of each union member's earnings to come to him or her as return on capital, and a smaller share as return on labor.

Offsetting Federal Deregulation by ESOP Bargaining

The philosophy of reduction of governmental involvement in the regulation of labor relations, like deregulation in other areas of business, can be accommodated in a market economy only by an increase in ESOP financing. Deregulation of industries like the airlines, trucking, and banking has strong public support because it tends to increase competition and lower consumer prices. There is a philosophical unity between the public rejection of union-supported redistribution and the deregulation of business and industry. In effect, many regulatory structures protected industry and union fixing of labor prices at levels that would have been radically lower had competition existed. This facilitated the packing of employees' wages and salaries with welfare. Deregulation often restores competition and forces employers to reduce wages and salaries to stay in business.

However, to reduce income redistribution without opening the way for employees to earn more by becoming capital workers is simply to accelerate forces that will lead to social and economic breakdown. To insist that people must earn their living under free-market conditions is eminently reasonable—but only if they can do so in ways consistent with the contemporary facts of production.

Voting of Stock Acquired through Two-Factor Financing

Each of the basic rights of a stockholder—to vote his stock in all matters where stockholder decision is necessary or desirable and to fully and regularly collect the wages of his capital—needs to be jealously protected and diligently exercised if the benefits of the private property system are to be democratized. This does not necessarily mean that stockholders or beneficial stockholders should try to assert their rights to vote a share of stock before it has been paid for by two-factor financing. It should be interpreted to mean that as stock is paid for, on a share-by-share basis, the voting power of the stockholder or beneficial stockholder should be activated. In the same vein, shares of stock purchased by an ESOP in connection with a particular financing transaction should not become votable by the beneficial owner before debt incurred in that transaction has been fully or substantially amortized. Lenders frequently insist that conditions existing at the time their loan is made continue until the debt is amortized. Normally, this is accomplishable within three to six years, but as the democratization of the economy proceeds, such financing periods should be greatly reduced. In any event, it is reasonable for financing creditors to take the steps they think necessary to assure the satisfactory performance of the loan amortization schedule. The specific temporary restrictions on the voting of shares in the process of their being acquired will vary from case to case. Even under commercially insured capital credit, Congress, the financing institutions, and the producers' unions themselves will doubtless have to address this subject.

Full and Periodic Payment of Capital Wages

Corporations do not even approach their potential usefulness in a democratized capitalist economy unless capital wages—the full corporate net earnings after operating reserves only and with no capital plow-in—are paid periodically and regularly with the same dependability as the wages of labor. Nothing less would enable the economy to eliminate inflation, prevent future inflation, and achieve an acceptable rate of economic growth. Furthermore, anything less fails to put capital work on a parity with labor work vis-à-vis participation in production and property integrity. For producers' unions to be fully effective in policing the full payout of capital wages, the national economic policy must be reinterpreted in terms of two factors, stockholders' rights to such full current payout must be accorded judicial or legislative recognition, and commercially insured capital credit for financing corporate economic growth must be made available. Nothing less than growth in their capital worker earnings, commensurate with the rate of technological progress, would justify employee and producers' unions' acceptance of stabilized labor work earnings, except for merit raises. Producer unions would be in a good position to represent their members against any corporation that seeks to cut corners by slighting their stockholder rights. The ultimate weapon in many such cases would be a class action on their behalf in the court of the appropriate jurisdiction.

Congress has already laid the groundwork for enforcing the full payout of capital wages with the enactment of the provisions of the Employee Stock Ownership Act of 1983 as part of the Deficit Reduction Act of 1984. Under that act, dividends paid on stock held for employees in ESOP trusts (capital wages) are deductible for corporate income tax purposes exactly like labor wages. Such dividends are required to be paid over to the beneficial owners of the stock, just like their labor wages.

Financing Corporate Growth

One of the motivating strengths of ESOP financing is the assurance, achieved differently for each particular corporation, that part or all of the corporation's future growth will be financed through the ESOP. This is important if the corporation is to gain the benefits of simulfinancing. It is equally important to assure lifetime employment for corporate and union employees. It is vital to minimize corporate production costs and maximize the rate of corporate growth. Finally, it is of basic importance to the economy itself to assure that the production of goods and services has the constant and open-ended support of consumers equipped with earnings to use in the marketplace. Only the well-planned and continuous synchronicity between the production of goods and services and the consumption of those goods and services will eliminate the massive waste and minimize the gyrations of the business cycle. The foregoing arguments equally apply to the financing of acquisitions. Here, too, the producers' union should be vigilant in assuring the financing of corporate acquisitions through the employer's ESOP, thus building ownership of the resulting corporate capital into the employees.

Diversifying an ESOP Portfolio: Pros and Cons

It has long been considered wise for a fiduciary or trustee to invest the employees' accounts in a substantial number of different assets, thus assuring that if the value of one or more of the investments should diminish or disappear, all would not be lost. This viewpoint in U.S. trust and banking fiduciary circles arose from economists' and lawyers' misinterpretation of the decision of the Massachusetts Supreme Court in the 1830 case of *Harvard College and Massachusetts General Hospital v. Francis Amory*, IX Pickering, 446.

In that case an attempt was made to charge the trustees of Harvard College Foundation with personal liability for the shrinkage in the value of its assets on the ground that they had been negligent in their investments on behalf of the foundation. The Supreme Court of Massachusetts wisely held that the liability of the trustees would have to be measured against the standard of a "reasonably prudent man" investing his own funds with a view to optimizing the income and preserving the principal. The court concluded that any reasonably prudent man in such circumstances would diversify his investments among a number of assets, each being selected for its soundness, but with the added assurance that if some investments did poorly, at least every reasonable effort to protect the aggregate value and earning power of the fund would have been made.

It came to be almost universally held that trustees of pension and profit sharing funds must diversify the trust investments in accordance with this *prudent man rule*. But this overlooks the fact that there are really two prudent man rules: one for the rich minority and the other for the capitalless masses who would like to become capital owners. The Supreme Court of Massachusetts was laying down a rule for already capitalized individuals and for fiduciaries who manage their assets. The problem before the court was: How should a trustee invest the trust's funds to keep the rich man rich, perhaps even to perpetuate the warehousing and protection of his morbid capital. Two-factor economics reveals that the real problem facing pension and profit sharing trustees is the reverse of that involved in the Massachusetts decision. Their duty is to help the capitalless become owners of significant capital holdings through using a different and more appropriate prudent man's rule—the *poor man's prudent man rule*. This tells capitalless individuals that the only legitimate way they can climb from poverty to capital ownership, if they can do it at all, is to invest in one sound enterprise. This was Andrew Carnegie's advice to the poor young man who wanted to get ahead in business: " 'Don't put all your eggs in one basket' is all wrong. I tell you, 'put all your eggs in one basket, and then watch that basket.' "[3] Only when corporate employees have acquired enough capital assets to justify diversification and to risk the conversion of their primary stock holdings into low-yield, secondhand securities does the *rich man's prudent man rule* begin to make any sense for them.

Since the nonresidential capital ownership in the U.S. economy has historically been lodged in the top 5 percent of wealthholders (except during the three to four decades following the first Homestead Acts in 1862), it must be obvious that making capital workers out of capitalless people has not been facilitated by pension and profit sharing. Quite the contrary. By applying the rich man's prudent man rule to capitalless working people, pension and profit sharing have contributed to keeping the capitalless working people capitalless, and even to making them poorer still by wasting their assets (now totaling well over $1 trillion) to generate fees and commissions.

Even the exceptions to this generalization involve cases where the fiduciaries disregarded the conventional wisdom and invested primarily in the securities of the employer—normally its common stock. However, the securities in these cases *are not* acquired in two-factor financing transactions, with the benefits of simulfinancing, but involve the purchasing of the employer's own stocks in the secondhand securities markets, where its key executives and shareholders are the sellers. The average 5 to 8 percent yield of assets held by pension and profit sharing trusts is but a fraction of the 20 to 40 or 50 percent pre-tax yield that managements insist on getting from the operating assets they purchase for the corporations themselves. ESOPs and other two-factor financing methods connect employees, through stock ownership, with that 20 to 50 percent pre-tax yield of assets to the corporate employer.

It is perfectly clear, however, that upon retirement from the labor-worker world, or other separation from employment, the individual, with guidance from both his employer and his producers' union, should evaluate and consider diversifying his or her holding of employer's stock. Producers' unions should also lobby Congress and the state governments for changes in the relevant laws and regulations to permit easy, tax-free rollover of ESOP accounts between the ESOP trusts of a former employer and a new employer when an employee changes jobs.

Questions Frequently Asked about ESOPs

Can ESOPs enable employees to expand their earning power? To the extent that one's labor involves effort in a market economy, increased earnings call for increased productive input. But to the extent that an employee also becomes a *capital worker*, one who engages in production through his ownership of corporate stock representing producing assets, his increased earning power is relatively vicarious.

But that is not the whole story. Increased compensation for labor is a business cost; it enters into the price of the products sold by the corporation. Progressively higher labor costs mean progressively higher product prices, which translates into inflation and loss of markets to lower cost foreign competitors. On the other hand, increased production and earnings as a capital worker do not raise product costs. Earnings or profits paid into ESOPs by employers are a residue or result, after costs of production have been computed, even though they are tax deductible by the corporation. Thus $1,000 in wage or salary increases would raise the price of the company's products by $1,000. But $1,000 paid into an employee's ESOP account does not, provided the employee understands that he is trading the acquisition of capital-produced income for the right to demand a higher than competitive wage or salary.

Since the primary source for increased production and increased corporate income is technological improvement and increased investment in productive assets, employee stockholders are better off using their ESOPs to bring them higher earnings that do not raise product prices than receiving increased pay and surrendering market advantage for their own corporation to lower price competitors. Said another way, if employee owners and their producers' unions understand the invisible structure of their corporations, it becomes a weapon in their hands to increase the corporation's market share, to raise the corporation's net earnings or profits, to raise the value of the stock they own, and to raise their combined earnings as labor and capital workers, even while producing lower priced goods and services for market.

Does the ESOP Eliminate the Distinction between Management and Non-Management Employees?

No. Management is an art that requires special aptitude, special skills, special education, and special experience. The suitability and competence of each management employee, like the suitability and competence of each non-management employee for his or her particular job, heavily influence the corporation's profitability and competitiveness. The effect of managerial incompetence may often be more far-reaching and destructive to a company's profitability than that of sub-managerial incompetence.

Where employees are stockholders, they become the most knowledgable of stockholders, for they are in a position to appraise each other's performance and the performance of management workers. All employee stockholders have a vital and legitimate interest in the professional qualifications of management to manage, just as they have an interest in the qualifications of each fellow employee to do an expert job. They can be of invaluable assistance both directly and through their producers' unions in representing their interest.

Are ESOPs Primarily for Financing Ailing Corporations?

No, they are not. It is the other way around. Failure of corporations to have adequate employee ownership is a major cause of corporate failure. Employees are their employer corporation's natural stockholders, for they have the greatest present and future stake in making the company profitable, in giving it the best possible image with its customers and with the public, and in having its products satisfy, as to quality and price, both domestic and foreign markets at the expense of competitors.

Do Employee Stockholders Really Need Producers' Unions?

They do indeed. But only if those unions understand the invisible structure of ESOP corporations and what it means to employee stockholders. This calls for an expansion of the jurisdiction and capabilities of unions so that they can represent their members both as labor workers and as capital workers. Producers' unions should help their members to lower employer costs, including labor costs, as those costs are reflected in product prices and therefore in corporate competitiveness. But at the same time, producers' unions should counsel their members to acquire progressively more capital ownership as the enterprises grow and to increase their incomes as capital workers, for the obvious reason that the purposes for engaging in production are to earn higher incomes, gain legitimate leisure, and to be better consumers. Producers' unions—the dual-worker unions—must follow through and see that their members become lifelong producers.

Can ESOP Companies Increase Employment of Labor Workers?

Yes, they can. When American companies, using ESOPs, can undersell their foreign competitors and out-perform them in product quality, millions of currently unemployed people will be needed to meet the enlarged and legitimate consumer demand for better, lower priced American goods and services. At the same time, our own dual-income producers will have rising purchasing power to buy more of the domestically produced goods and services. Furthermore, by making capital workers of labor workers as technology advances, we will retain our advantage. There is no mystery as to what enables a business to conquer its competitors—it is by producing and marketing higher quality products at lower cost. Virtually every U.S. corporation, with the proper invisible structure that includes ESOPs, can out-perform foreign competitors in

U.S. markets and do so while providing the highest incomes for American consumers.

The tougher problem will be out-performing foreign competitors in their own markets. We have always had this power, but we have not used it. Instead, we have maximized the ability of absentee capital owners, who number less than 5 percent of the total population and who are not labor workers in the companies where they are capital workers, to be ever more irresponsible to their corporations as their stock ownership grows. We now must correct this formula for disaster through intensive and broad use of ESOPs and other two-factor financing methods.

How Do Employees Market Their ESOP-Acquired Stock?

Skillfully and professionally designed ESOPs include internal stock markets properly funded to buy employee-owned stock at fair values appraised under the valuation regulations of the U.S. Treasury and Labor Departments. These values are far more reliable and favorable to stockholders than are the public stock markets, where stock values are routinely depressed except in the midst of takeover raids.[4] By selling their stock, usually at retirement or separation from employment, to the ESOP's own private stock market, employee stockholders are able to diversify into other securities, annuities, and so on, in accordance with the plan's provisions, or they may choose to liquidate shares in order to use their value to live on. Proper ESOP design of the invisible structure of employee-owned companies makes the internal stock market for each corporation's own stock just as important as the ESOP itself.

Is Employee Ownership of Stock through ESOPs Similar to European Co-determination?

No, it is not. Co-determination was first introduced into Europe in Germany, following World War II. It has since spread to many European Common Market economies. It involves extensive labor union participation in management decisionmaking and, in some cases, collective union ownership of stock, but no capitalization of individual employees. Thus it does not democratize the economic power represented by the capital of the employer. Co-determination, as practiced in European companies, mixes political decisions with business decisions and often gives corporate employees the worst of both possible worlds: participation in management by amateur and unqualified people and no power or opportunity to become capital workers or to attain lifetime employment. American corporations with substantial ESOP employee ownership have a competitive edge over corporations whose invisible structures are heavily influenced by co-determination.

NOTES

1. "How the Institutions Rule the Market," *New York Times*, November 24, 1984, sec. 3, p. 1.
2. *Wall Street Journal*, September 28, 1984, p. 3.
3. Andrew Carnegie, *The Empire of Business* (New York: Doubleday, Page & Co., 1902), p. 17.
4. Corporations in which employees, through an ESOP, have a controlling interest in their stock, an ESOP-minded management, and employee representation by a producers' union are as hostile-takeover proof as a corporation can be.

Glossary

Binary Economics: Adam Smith's free market theory, with its central assumption modified to reflect that, since the Industrial Revolution, people produce goods and services and earn income both through their labor power and their privately owned capital.

Boondoggle: Commonly defined as pointless, unnecessary work, we use the term to mean work or labor worker jobs that would not exist in a democratized capitalist economy. Such work or jobs exist only to give the appearance of economic legitimacy to income payments that are in reality welfare, either because the product would be unmarketable or worthless to consumers who spend their own incomes under free-market conditions or because the product itself would not even be produced. We also use the term to cover the portion of a product's value that exceeds the price of its free-market competitive value by the amount of labor welfare packed into it. Most boondoggle is government subsidized, either directly or indirectly, through contracts with private enterprise. In both cases the cost of the disguised welfare is coercively borne by taxpayers or coercively packed into the price of goods and services and paid for by consumers as though it were an actual cost of production.

Capital Worker: One who engages in economic production and earns income through his or her privately owned capital. A capital worker is not generally required to be personally present at the scene of production, although astute management of the ownership interest in capital is constantly required.

Capitalist Democracy: See *Democratic Capitalist Economy*.

Capitalized: Owning capital; legitimately equipped with capital through purchasing and paying for it.

Collateralization Principle: *Collateralization* occurs when an individual borrows money to buy newly issued stock and mortgages, pledges, or hypothecates the newly purchased assets, and often other assets, to doubly guarantee repayment of the acquisition credit. Collateralization serves an insurance function in a capital acquisition transaction, insuring against the risk that the acquired asset may not pay for itself within the agreed time period, as contemplated by the feasibility plan.

Not only is collateralization a crude, inefficient, and enormously expensive way of insuring the feasibility risk in capital financing, but there are decisive economic and political arguments against it. It limits access to credit to buy capital to those who already own substantial amounts of capital and who can, in effect, self-insure the feasibility risk. The practice of requiring collateralization is the chief cause of capital morbidity (see *Morbid Capital*). The *economic function* of collateralization, from every logical aspect, is a casualty insurance issue. We call such insurance *capital diffusion insurance*. Not only is casualty insurance in general the oldest of the financial arts, but the cost of such insurance is minimized by competition and is constantly adjusted to market experience.

COMCOP (Commercial Capital Ownership Plan): See pages 88 to 92.

CSOP (Consumer Stock Ownership Plan): See pages 67 to 72.

Democratic Capitalist Economy: A national political economy characterized by an economic democracy within a political democracy. Such a political economy may also be properly called a *social capitalist* economy.

Economic Autonomy: The words *autonomy* or *autonomous* are normally used in connection with political power since civilization is unaccustomed, up to this point, to treating social power as a composite of political and economic power. We use the words *autonomy* and *autonomous* in their economic context to characterize individuals or families that are economically self-sufficient, that is, able to earn sufficient income by their participation in production, usually as concurrent labor workers and capital workers, to support the standard of living which they reasonably choose for themselves.

Economic Democracy: Democracy is a form of government under which social power is held by the individual citizens. The major components of social power are political and economic power. Political power is the power to participate, to a degree accepted as reasonable, in the making, interpreting, administering, and enforcing of the laws. Economic power is the power to produce goods and services; it is the power to earn income through engaging in the production of goods or services for purchase by consumers in the marketplace. One can legitimately engage in production either through personally owned labor power or privately owned capital. As technological advance changes the way in which goods and services are produced from labor intensive to capital intensive, economic democracy cannot be achieved or sustained except through the democratic ownership of capital. In bringing about democratic ownership of capital, the state (i.e., the federal government) must act as surrogate for nature's democratization of labor power.

Encapitalized: See *Capitalized*.

ESOP (Employee Stock Ownership Plan): See pages 51 to 55; also 59 to 66.

Feasibility Principle: Relates to the self-financing nature of capital. It is the reasonable expectation of experienced people seeking to acquire capital assets that the capital in question will pay for itself, that is, earn sufficient net income to repay its equity costs of acquisition within a planned period of time (the rule of thumb in business is three to five years). Thereafter it will continue to produce income for its owners indefinitely, its productive power preserved by proper maintenance, depreciation policies, and research and development funding, all of which are expensed before net income is computed. *Feasibility is the basic logic of capital acquisition in the business world.*

Full Employment: "A state of the economy in which all persons who want to work can find employment without much difficulty at prevailing rates of pay. Some unemployment, both voluntary and involuntary, is not incompatible with full employment, since allowances must be made for frictional and seasonal factors which are always present to some degree. In the U.S., a figure of 4% is generally taken as the normal rate of such temporary unemployment, and this figure is thus also considered the maximum permissible unemployment level for a full-employment situation." (*The McGraw-Hill Dictionary of Modern Economics,* 2nd Edition.) Within the logic of democratic capitalist economics *full employment* refers to an economy in which every mature individual or consumer unit is at all times engaged in production of a reasonably satisfactory standard of living, as a labor worker, as a capital worker, or concurrently as both.

GSOP (General Stock Ownership Plan): See pages 75 to 83.

ICOP (Individual Capital Ownership Plan): See pages 85 to 88.

Invisible Structure: The economic rights and obligations, privileges and duties of individuals, based upon laws, contracts, or customs that connect particular people with other people and with assets within a particular economy. The invisible structure determines who owns what in the visible economy. A rational invisible structure is indispensable to a rational economy.

Labor Worker: An individual who engages in economic production and earns income by employing his or her physical and mental abilities.

Limitation Principle: The idea, derived from both the common law of property and the logic of free-market economics articulated by Adam Smith, that the sole purpose of production is consumption by the producers, and that therefore a household should not acquire or hold more capital productive power than it requires to earn the income it chooses to devote to consumption. See pages 24 to 29; also *Morbid Capital.*

Market Democracy or Free-Market Democracy: A free-market economy in which social power, comprised of political and economic power, is democratically held by individual citizens.

Morbid Capital: That part of a capital holding or estate of an individual or family that produces income over and above that desired and used to defray the costs of the individual's or family's self-chosen standard of living. Such excess productive power violates the common law limitations inherent in private property because, without benefitting its owner, it beggars others by depriving them of adequate economic opportunity—economic autonomy. Morbid capital is contrary to the public interest because it results in strife and suffering and is economically undemocratic. See also *Limitation Principle.*

MUSOP (Mutual Stock Ownership Plan): See pages 66 to 67.

New Unions: See *Producers' Unions.*

One-Factor Economics: Any economic concept that regards labor or service work as the only way for individuals to participate in production and earn income. Implicitly, one-factor economic concepts treat capital (land, structures, machines, and capital intangibles, normally represented by common stock) as a catalytic agent, rather than as assets through which capital owners can participate in production and earn income. One-factor economists regard capital as the agent that raises the mythical "productivity" of workers who work with it but own none of it. These economists and their adherents believe that it makes no difference who owns the capital, so long as there is plenty of it.

Participation Principle: The idea that the only *economically* legitimate way to acquire income is to participate in production sufficiently to earn it under competitive conditions. In a preindustrial era this could be done through labor alone, but in an industrial era participation in both labor and capital work is required by all except money-making geniuses. See page 24.

Private Property: The sum total of rights which an individual, as owner, holds in a thing he or she owns. See pages 23 to 24.

Private-Property, Free-Market, Capitalist Democracy: See *Democratic Capitalist Economy.*

Producers' Unions: Employee unions, ordinarily established as labor unions, that have expanded their functions and goals to comprehend all participation in production, both as labor workers and as capital workers.

Property Principle: See *Private Property.*

PUBCOP (Public Capital Ownership Plan): See pages 92 to 95.

RECOP (Residential Capital Ownership Plan): See pages 99 to 103.

Say's Law: See Chapter 4.

Secondhand Securities: Securities not acquired upon original issue but from sellers in secondary markets. Secondhand securities cannot be acquired through transactions in which the simulfinancing advantages are achieved jointly by corporate issuers and stock purchasers.

Simulfinancing: The purchase by individuals of original or newly issued corporate stock through a two-factor financing method. In such transactions, each investment simultaneously purchases assets for the corporation and stock ownership for the individual buyers. Each of the two-factor financing techniques, except RECOP financing, which does not require a corporate vehicle, employs simulfinancing.

Social Power: The composite of political power and economic power—the two major components of power held and exercised by individual citizens in a democratic capitalist economy.

Social Revolution: The process by which the ideas of the well-capitalized few become the ideas of the capitalless many. Revolution in this sense does not imply force or violence.

Two-Factor Economy: A private-property, free-market economy operating on the assumption that individuals or consumer families may participate in production and earn income by employing, or having others employ, their privately owned labor power or their privately owned capital (land, structures, machines, or capital intangibles, normally represented by capital stock), or, in the most usual case, in both capacities.

Index

"Adequate earning power," 88
Affluence, 7, 8, 16, 18, 25, 114, 115, 145, 147
AFL-CIO, 141, 142
Aggregate consumer income, 32, 33–34
Agrarian economy, 18
Agricultural capital, 19
Alaskan General Stock Ownership
    Corporation (AGSOC), 76–81
Ardrey, Robert, 99
Aristotle, 85, 137
Artists and musicians, 28, 37
Asset-based finance, 42–43

Baker, Howard, 110
Beard, Charles, 13–14
Blake, William, 51
Boondoggle, 37, 165
BP Pipeline, Inc., 76, 78
British Petroleum Company, 79
Burke, Kenneth, 117
Business corporations, 19, 69
    democratizing, 117–131
Business cycle, 21, 26, 158
Business risk. *See* Feasibility risk

Capital acquisition by the
    undercapitalized, 51–52
Capital-cost recovery cycle, 43, 44
Capital credit, 39–40, 46, 47, 51
Capital credit access, 112–113, 115
Capital credit insurance, 41
Capital credit risk. *See* Feasibility risk
Capital diffusion insurance, 164
Capital Diffusion Reinsurance Corporation
    (CDRC), 108, 109, 111
Capital state, 27–28
Capital facilities, 92

Capital financing mechanisms, 55–57,
    96–97
Capital formation and acquisition, 43–45
Capital gifts, 27, 28
Capital in the American Economy: Its
    Formation and Financing, 39
Capital instruments, 39
Capital-intensive production, 6, 7, 19, 20,
    35, 46, 129, 167
Capital morbidity, 20, 25, 33, 35, 36–38,
    89, 90, 92, 128–129, 166, 168
Capital ownership, 7, 8–9, 14–15, 16, 19,
    25–26, 29, 40, 147, 148, 167
Capital plow-in, 127, 157
Capital power, 8–9, 122
Capital productiveness, 7, 8, 16–17, 19, 33,
    124–131, 143, 144, 148
Capital wages, 29, 121, 157
Capital work/capital workers, 7, 8, 9, 17,
    29, 34, 40, 46, 47, 89, 123, 124, 139, 145,
    148, 157, 165
    emigration of jobs, 154–155
Carnation Corporation, 154
Carnegie, Andrew, 4, 15, 159
Casualty insurance, 40–41, 166
Charity, 27, 37
Chrysler Corporation, 41, 110
Clark, John Bates, 151
Class action suits, 154, 157
Co-determination, 163–164
Collateralization principle, 42, 165–166
Commercial banks, 106–107
Commercial capital credit insurance, 93,
    105–115, 128
Commercial Capital Ownership Plan
    (COMCOP), 56, 88–92
Commercial real estate, 88, 89

Common law of private property, 24, 27, 36, 123, 168
Common law trust, 106
Competence, 4, 29, 114
Constituency trusts, 61, 69, 88, 106, 130
Constitutional rights, 12–14, 19, 20, 21, 24
Construction industry, 89
Consumer credit, 40
Consumer demand, 20, 40, 44–45
Consumer income, 17, 28, 44–45
Consumer purchasing power, 40
Consumer Stock Ownership Plan (CSOP), 9, 56, 67–72
Continental Illinois Bank, 41, 110
Corporate growth, financing, 157–158
Corporate ownership, 19
Corporate taxation, 89, 90, 125

Death, 27
Debt financing, 42
Deficit Reduction Act (1984), 157
Deindustrialization, 120–121
Democracy, 11, 12
Democratic capitalism, 23–29
Democratic capitalist economy, 19–21, 166
Depressions, panics, and recessions, 26, 34, 111
Donahue, Thomas R., 142
Double-entry bookkeeping, 20, 25, 33, 36
Douglas, William O., 75
Durant, Will and Ariel, 16

Economic alienation, 122, 148
Economic autonomy, 6, 20, 29, 93, 166, 168
Economic democracy, 11, 12, 14, 18, 26, 166–167
Economic equality, 14
Economic growth, 90
Economic instability, 26, 34, 37
Economic opportunity, 31, 32–33, 115
Economic policy, 110, 118–119, 122–124
  corporate and national, 119–120
Economic power, 11, 12, 13, 14, 18, 19, 115, 166–167
Economic process, 11
Ellis, Havelock, 135
Employee "leasing," 95
Employee Stock Ownership Act (1984), 62, 65, 112–113, 157
Employee Stock Ownership Plan (ESOP), 8, 9, 51, 52–55, 59–66, 149, 151–164

Employment Act (1946), 122–123
England, 136
European Common Market, 163
Excess capital income, 25, 26, 34–35, 36

Fabricated capital, 25
Feasibility principle, 167
Feasibility risk, 42, 44, 105, 166
Federal Deposit Insurance Corporation, 41
Federal Farm Credit Banks, 41, 110
Federal Reserve Bank, 41, 93, 108
Federal Savings and Loan Insurance Corporation, 41
Finance, conventional, 39–47
Financial Security Assurance, Inc., 41
Foreign competition, 162–163
Foreign investment, 154–155
Free market economy, 11–12, 17, 168
Frontier, 16, 18
Full employment, 5, 6, 7, 89, 118–119, 135, 167
Function-based financing vehicles, 55–56. *See also* Consumer Stock Ownership Plan; Employee Stock Ownership Plan; Mutual Stock Ownership Plan
Funding source, immediate/ultimate, 106

General Stock Ownership Corporation Law (1978), 76
General Stock Ownership Plan (GSOP), 9, 56, 75–83
Germany, 136, 163
Gompers, Samuel, 142, 144
Gotha Programme, 136–137
Government deregulation, 155–156
Government intervention, 34, 41, 109–112
Government regulation, 34, 97
Greed/love of power, 29, 37, 38
Grey Advertising, 16
Gross national product, 32, 33, 144
Grosscup, Peter S., 4, 17–18, 19

Hamilton, Alexander, 14
Hanson Trust (U.K.), 154
Harrington, J., 12
Harvard College and Massachusetts General Hospital v. *Francis Amory* (1830), 158
Homestead Acts (1862), 16, 19, 159
Housing finance, 99–103, 113
Howe, Irving, 26
Human rights, 12, 24, 56

Income distribution, 25, 32, 33, 34
Income redistribution, 7, 8, 18, 20, 24, 37,
    40, 93, 110, 111, 112, 125, 128, 144, 149
    and deregulation, 155–156
Income taxation, deferred, 62
Individual Capital Ownership Plan
    (ICOP), 56, 85–88
Individual ownership, 19
Industrial capital, 15, 19
Industrial policy, 110
Industrialization, 15, 18–19, 33, 35, 136
Inflation, 26, 100, 111, 128, 147
Infrastructure. *See* Public Capital
    Ownership Plan
Insuring business risk, 40–43
Interest rates, 40, 100
Internal cash-flow financing, 42
Internal stock markets, 65, 163
Investment decision, 43–44
Investor market versus speculator
    markets, 81–82
Invisible structure, 45–47, 168

Japan, 124
Jefferson, Thomas, 14
"Job security" measures, 148

Kelso, Louis O., 52, 53
Kelso, Louis O., and Mortimer J. Adler, 42
Keynes, Maynard, 33
Kirkland, Lane, 142
Kuznets, Simon, 39, 46–47

Labor demand, 15, 17
Labor-intensive production, 6, 19, 20, 35,
    46, 167
Labor laws, 8
Labor power, 5–6, 14, 122, 167
Labor price, 17, 111
Labor productiveness, 14, 15, 16–17, 19
Labor productivity myth, 5, 8, 120,
    127–128, 138, 143, 144, 148, 169
Labor theory of value, 5–6
Labor unions, 8, 135–139, 141–149
Labor "value," 15, 17, 18
Labor wages, 29, 120–121, 144, 146, 157
Labor work/labor workers, 7, 17, 28–29,
    46, 89, 123, 124, 139, 148, 157, 168
Land ownership, 13–14, 15, 16, 18, 19
Le Corbusier, 99
Lesher, Richard L., 141

Lessons of History, 16
Lifetime employment, 63, 65, 93, 95, 124,
    158
Limitation principle, 24–29, 168
Lincoln, Abraham, 105
Living standards, 28, 142
Lockheed Corporation, 41, 110
Long, Russell, 53

Madison, James, 13
Malthus, Thomas, 136
Management, 145, 161
Martial, 39
Marx, Karl, 138
Massachusetts Supreme Court, 158, 159
Meany, George, 146
Mergers, acquisitions, and leveraged
    buyouts, 8–9, 121
Monetary stability, 28
Monopolistic/oligopolistic consumer
    relationships, 69
Monsanto Company, 155
Mortgage credit, 100
Mortgage insurance, 41
Municipal debt securities insurance, 41
Mutual Stock Ownership Plan (MUSOP),
    56, 66–67

National Center for Employee Ownership,
    131
National Labor Relations Board, 142
Natural law, 27
Nestle S.A. (Switz.), 154
New Capitalists, 42
New Deal, 109, 111, 125
New York City
    bailout, 41, 110
    Harlem/Bedford-Stuyvesant, 95
Nonresidential capital ownership, 16, 42,
    46, 88, 127, 159

O'Mahoney, Joseph C., 11
One-factor economy, 90, 105, 118, 142–149,
    168–169

Participation principal, 24, 169
Peninsula Newspaper (Palo Alto, Calif.),
    52–53
Pension funds, 152, 159, 160
Political democracy, 11, 12, 14
Political equality, 13–14

Political power, 11, 12, 13, 166
Political process, 11
Plutocratic capitalism, 18–19, 21, 115, 144
Portfolio diversification, 65, 86, 158–160
Positive law, 27
Poverty, relativity of, 114–115
Preemption laws, 19
Price system, 110
Private property, 169
Producers' unions, 139, 142–146, 169
Product costs, 160–161
Production-consumption gap, 5, 31
Production ethic, 6–7
Production factors, primary/secondary, 29
Production process, 6–7
Productive autonomy, 145
Productive power of capital, 8–9
Profit sharing, 146, 159, 160
Property principle, 23–24, 169
Property rights, 12–14, 19, 20, 27
Property transfers, 27, 28
Public Capital Ownership Plan (PUBCOP), 56, 92–95, 121–122
Public pensions, 95, 122
Public policy, 27, 56
   and legislation, 122–124
Public sector, privatization of, 92
Public utilities, 69, 70–72, 85
Purchasing power, 32, 34
Puritan ethic, 6–7

Reagan administration, 141, 142, 147
Real capital, 129, 130
Real estate lobbies, 89, 90
Redevelopment, 95–96
Residential Capital Ownership Plan (RECOP), 56–57, 99–103, 112, 113
Retirement income, 124
Reuther, Walter, 145–146
Revenue Act (1978), 79
Rich-poor gap, 3, 15, 16
Roosevelt, Franklin D., 5, 23, 111

Savings-based financing, 8, 15, 41, 47, 113–114, 115, 128
Say, Jean Baptiste, 31
Say's Law of Markets, 31–38
G.D. Searle & Co., 155
Securities markets, secondary, 81–82, 97, 152, 160, 169
Self-financing, 43, 167

Self-insurance, 41–42, 105, 166
Simulfinancing, 47, 61–62, 130–131, 151, 158, 169–170
Sitting Bull, 5
Skills, 17
Slavery, 14, 18, 25
Small-business financing, 86
Smith, Adam, 31, 119, 168
Social injustice, 25–26
Social power, 11, 18, 115, 166, 168, 170
Socialist movement, 136–137
"Special improvement districts," 96
Speculators, 81, 82, 152
Stock, voting of, 156
Stock distribution to workers, 145–146
Stockholding constituencies, 66
Subsistence, 7, 18, 149
Sufficiency, 4
Suffrage, 12, 13
Sumner, William Graham, 3
Supply and demand, 31, 34
Supply-side economics, 44
Sweden, 144

Taxation, 40, 89, 90, 93, 110, 111, 125
Technological change, 6, 15, 16–19, 33, 114, 144, 147, 148
Tennessee Valley Authority, 97
Toynbee, Arnold, 15
TransAlaska Pipeline Service Corporation (TAPS), 78, 79
Transfer payments. See Income redistribution
Trickle-down theory, 111, 115
Two-factor economy, 51, 54, 65–66, 89, 105, 169–170

Unemployment, 147, 149, 154, 162, 167
Union decertification elections, 141
United Auto Workers, 148
United Nations, 144
United States
   Constitution/Declaration of
      Independence, 13, 14, 33, 36, 72, 124
   labor/capital contributions to GNP, 144
   Postal Service, 97
U.S. Industries, 154

Valley Nitrogen Producers, Inc., 67, 72
Vandalism, arson, and pilferage, 122, 128
Vocational education, 147

Wages/benefits, "concessionary
    reductions" in, 142
Washington, George, 18
Wealth concentration, 8, 14–15, 35, 46, 121,
    144
Wealth of Nations, 119

Webster, Daniel, 12
Welfare, 24, 28, 37, 40, 44, 45, 93, 111, 115,
    120, 127, 147
Whitney, Byrl, 143
Work-time loss, 129
Working conditions, 147

About the Authors

Louis O. Kelso originated the species of capital acquisition financing techniques of which the Employee Stock Ownership Plan (ESOP) is the best known. In 1958 his theory of free-market, private-property economics was published in *The Capitalist Manifesto*, coauthored with philosopher Mortimer J. Adler. In 1967 he and Patricia Hetter Kelso published *Two-Factor Theory: The Economics of Reality*. Since 1970 the Kelsos have devoted virtually all of their time and efforts to establishing Kelso & Company as an investment banking firm specializing in ESOP financing. They now concentrate on advancing the adoption of the seven other capital financing methods, changing the national economic policy, and introducing two-factor economic policies and investment banking methods into other developed and developing economies. Kelso holds the degrees of B.S. in finance, cum laude, and J.D. from the University of Colorado, where he was editor-in-chief of *The Rocky Mountain Law Review* and later taught constitutional law and municipal finance as an associate professor. A corporate and financial lawyer, he headed his own law firm in San Francisco from 1958 to 1975. In 1963 he was awarded the degree of honorary Doctor of Science in economics from Araneta University, Manila, The Philippines.

Patricia Hetter Kelso is a vice president of Kelso & Company and also vice president of the Institute for the Study of Economic Systems. For many years she worked in Stockholm as an international marketing specialist. She has coauthored with Louis Kelso *Two-Factor Theory: The Economics of Reality* as well as many articles, monographs, occasional papers, and congressional submissions. She holds a B.A. degree in government and philosophy from the University of Texas at Austin.